Rich Rewards
Treats for the Soul

*This book is dedicated to the memory of
my mother and to my father.
My mother, Eleanor Moore,
was a very talented baker and we owned
and operated a pastry shop together.
She was my teacher and mentor and
she inspired me to produce this book.*

*A special thank you to my husband, Glenn, and my children
Blaine, Shaun, and Scott for all their love and support.*

*Part of the proceeds from this book will be donated to
the Campbell River Hospice Society
and
the Medicine Hat Palliative*

by Heather E. Heughan

PICTURED ON THE FRONT COVER
Strawberry Almond Shortcake, page 33

rich rewards

by
Heather Heather

First Printing – July 1997

Rich Rewards Publishing
323 – 9 Street S.E.
Medicine Hat, Alberta
Canada T1A 1N4

Canadian Cataloguing in Publication Data

Heather, Heather, 1961-
Rich rewards

Includes index.

ISBN 1-895292-90-5

1. Desserts. I. Title

TX773.H43 1997   641.8'6   C97-920090-3

Photography by
Patricia Holdsworth
Patricia Holdsworth Photography,
Regina, Saskatchewan

Dishes and Accessories courtesy of:
Indigo, Regina, Saskatchewan
Terra Cotta Plus, Regina, Saskatchewan
Raku plate, page 71, by Donovan Chester

Designed, Printed, and Produced in Canada by:
Centax Books, a Division of PrintWest Communications Ltd.
Publishing Director, Photo Designer, and Food Stylist: Margo Embury
1150 Eighth Avenue, Regina, Saskatchewan, Canada S4R 1C9
(306) 525-2304   FAX (306) 757-2439

 2

Table of Contents

I wish to extend special thanks to Margo Embury of Centax Books for her expertise, guidance, and artistic input; to Iona Glabus, publishing assistant, for all her hard work; to Patricia Holdsworth for the wonderful photographs, and to all the others, too numerous to mention, whose hard work and support helped turn my dream into a reality.

baking Tips

- Use all-vegetable shortening rather than butter or margarine to grease baking pans and you will have fewer problems with sticking.

- Line the bottoms of cake pans with parchment or waxed paper for easier cake removal after baking.

- Chill bowl and beaters before whipping cream. Whipping cream should be well chilled.

- Egg whites at room temperature whip better than chilled egg whites.

- If buttermilk is unavailable try substituting soured milk. To sour 1 cup of milk put 1 tbsp. of lemon juice or vinegar in a 1 cup measure and fill with milk.

- When melting chocolate chips for the tops of bars, add a small spoonful of all-vegetable shortening; the mixture will be easier to spread.

- Never melt chocolate over high heat; it can turn lumpy or burn.

- Pipe excess whipping cream into rosettes and freeze for future use.

- For ease in cutting, score or mark the top of chocolate-covered bars or squares with a knife before the chocolate is completely set.

- To avoid excess crumbs when decorating cakes, try freezing the cakes before the icing is applied.

- If icing seems too stiff and hard to spread, decrease the amount of powdered sugar and increase the amount of margarine or butter used. This will also cut the sweetness.

- When decorating with food colorings, use dark colors sparingly and only for accents.

- Bake cookies on the middle rack of the oven.

- Heavy flat cookie sheets, without sides, allow for even air circulation and even baking. Bake only 1 sheet of cookies at a time, or if using 2 small pans, space at least 2" (5 cm) from the oven walls and each other.

- Cool cookies completely before storing to prevent sticking.

Cookies & Squares

Chocolate Caramel Thumbprint Treats

⅔ cup	white sugar
½ cup	butter, softened
1	egg, separated
2 tbsp.	milk
1 tsp.	vanilla
1 cup	all-purpose flour
⅓ cup	unsweetened cocoa
¼ tsp.	salt
1 cup	finely chopped pecans

Caramel filling:

⅔ cup	sweetened condensed milk (½ of a 10 oz. [300 mL] can)
½ cup	brown sugar
2 tbsp.	corn syrup
½ cup	butter

Topping:

½ cup	semisweet chocolate chips
1 tsp.	shortening

Beat sugar, butter, egg yolk, milk, and vanilla until well blended. Stir together flour, cocoa, and salt. Add to butter mixture; mix thoroughly. Chill dough at least 1 hour, or until firm enough to handle.

Preheat oven to 350°F and lightly grease cookie sheets. Shape dough into 1" balls. Dip each ball into beaten egg white and roll in pecans. Place balls 1" apart on cookie sheets. Using your thumb, make an indentation in the center of each ball. Bake in oven for 10-12 minutes, or until set.

Meanwhile, prepare the caramel filling. Combine all ingredients and cook over medium heat, stirring constantly, and bring to a gentle boil. Continue cooking for 5 minutes, stirring continuously. Remove from heat and let cool slightly (approximately 5 minutes) before using in cookies.

Remove cookies from oven and once again make a slight indentation in center of each cookie. Immediately spoon approximately ½ tsp. of caramel filling into the center of each cookie. Cool completely.

Heat the chocolate chips and shortening together until melted, stir until smooth and drizzle the chocolate mixture over the tops of the cookies.

Makes approximately 2½ dozen cookies.

reverse Chocolate Chunk Cookies

Chewy dark chocolate cookies have tempting chunks of white chocolate.

1½ cups	butter, softened
1 cup	white sugar
¾ cup	packed light brown sugar
1 tsp.	vanilla
2	eggs
2½ cups	all-purpose flour
⅔ cup	unsweetened cocoa
1 tsp.	baking soda
½ tsp.	salt
10 oz.	white chocolate chunks
½ cup	chopped pecans

Preheat oven to 350°F and lightly grease cookie sheets.

Cream butter and sugars until light. Add vanilla and eggs. Mix well. Combine flour, cocoa, baking soda, and salt. Stir into creamed mixture. Stir in chocolate chunks and pecans. Scoop out ¼ cup of cookie dough for each cookie and place 4" apart on cookie sheets. Flatten each cookie slightly. Bake 12-14 minutes, or until cookies are firm in the center. Cool for 5 minutes on cookie sheets then remove to wire rack and cool completely.

Makes approximately 2½ dozen large cookies. These cookies can be frozen.

PICTURED ON PAGE 17.

 ## White Chocolate

Rich and creamy tasting, white chocolate is not true chocolate. It is made of a mixture of cocoa butter, sugar, milk solids, lecithin, and vanilla. There is no chocolate liquor in it, and the flavor is very different from the various dark chocolates. Each type of chocolate has its devotees.

double Chocolate Chunk Cookies

A rich, chocolate-lover's cookie.

1 cup	butter, softened
1 cup	light brown sugar
½ cup	white sugar
2	eggs
2⅓ cups	all-purpose flour
1 tsp.	baking soda
½ tsp.	salt
5 oz.	milk chocolate chunks
5 oz.	semisweet chocolate chunks

Preheat oven to 375°F and lightly grease cookie sheets.

Cream butter and sugars until fluffy. Add eggs and beat well. Combine flour, baking soda, and salt. Add to creamed mixture, mixing until a stiff dough is formed. Stir in chocolate chunks. Scoop out ¼ cup of the dough for each cookie and place 4" apart on cookie sheets. Flatten each cookie slightly. Bake for 15 minutes, or until light golden brown.

Makes approximately 1½ dozen large cookies. These cookies can be frozen.

Scandinavian Thumbprint Cookies

Dots of jelly glow like jewels in these easy-to-make cookies.

½ cup	butter, softened
¼ cup	brown sugar
1	egg yolk, beaten
1 cup	flour
1	egg white, lightly beaten
½ cup	finely chopped nuts, pecans, almonds, OR walnuts
½ cup	raspberry jam OR jelly for filling

Scandinavian Thumbprint Cookies
Continued

Preheat oven to 350°F and lightly grease cookie sheets.

Cream butter and sugar. Beat in egg yolk and flour. Mix until smooth. Roll dough into balls, dip in egg white then in chopped nuts. Place balls on cookie sheets. Make an indentation in the center of each cookie. Place a small dab of jam or jelly in the indentation. Bake for 8-10 minutes.

Store in a covered container with waxed paper between cookie layers.

Makes approximately 18 cookies. These cookies can be frozen.

Shortbread Cookies

A favorite year round, this rich buttery cookie was traditionally served at Christmas and New Year's celebrations. The original round shape had notched edges to resemble the rays of the sun. Decorative molds are often used to create patterns on the baked, unmolded shortbread.

2 cups	**butter, softened**
1 cup	**berry sugar***
4 cups	**all-purpose flour**

Cream butter well. Add sugar a little at a time, beating well. Add flour, using hands to knead well. Shape into logs. Chill in refrigerator several hours or overnight.

Preheat oven to 325°F and lightly grease cookie sheets. Slice dough and place 1" apart on cookie sheets. Bake for 8-10 minutes, or until bottoms of cookies are light brown. Cool on wire racks.

Makes approximately 4 dozen cookies. These cookies freeze well.

* If berry or fruit sugar is unavailable put regular white sugar in a food processor, blend to break the granules into finer particles.

VARIATIONS: If ginger is one of your flavor passions, add ⅔ cup of chopped candied ginger to the dough to make spicy **Ginger Shortbread**. For **Orange or Lemon Shortbread,** add 4 tbsp. grated lemon or orange peel. To make **Apricot Shortbread**, add ⅔ cup chopped dried apricots.

almond Crescents

Also known as Greek Shortbread (Kourabiedes), these cookies literally melt in your mouth. In Greek homes a clove is often inserted in the top of these cookies at Christmas to denote the magi's gift of spices to the Christ child.

1 cup	butter, softened
⅓ cup	white sugar
½ tsp.	almond extract
1⅔ cups	all-purpose flour
⅔ cup	ground almonds
	powdered (icing) sugar

Cream butter, sugar, and flavoring until light. Add flour and nuts, mix well. Form into small crescents and place on ungreased cookie sheets. If dough is too sticky chill for 1 hour.

Preheat oven to 375°F. Bake for 8-10 minutes, or until light brown on bottom. Cool slightly then dust with powdered (icing) sugar. Cool completely. Store in a covered container with waxed paper between layers. Dust with powdered (icing) sugar before serving, if desired.

Makes approximately 3 dozen cookies. These cookies can be frozen.

PICTURED ON PAGE 17.

Swedish Cookies

These shortbread-style cookies have a lighter more delicate texture, and the added crunch of pecans.

2 cups	butter, softened
1 cup	powdered (icing) sugar
3½ cups	all-purpose flour
2 cups	chopped pecans
¼ tsp.	salt
	additional icing sugar for dusting cookies

Swedish Cookies
Continued

Cream butter and sugar until light. Add remaining ingredients, except for the additional icing sugar, and mix thoroughly. Chill for 1 hour.

Preheat oven to 350°F and lightly grease cookie sheets. Roll dough into 1" balls and place 1" apart on cookie sheets. Bake for 8-10 minutes. Cool completely on wire racks. When balls are cool, sprinkle with additional powdered (icing) sugar.

Makes approximately 3½ dozen cookies. These cookies can be frozen.

Christmas Cookies

These shortbread-style cookies have a softer texture than regular shortbread cookies.

1 cup	**powdered (icing) sugar**
1 cup	**butter, softened**
1	**egg**
1 tsp.	**vanilla**
2½ cups	**all-purpose flour**
1 cup	**chopped, mixed red and green cherries**

Combine sugar, butter, egg, and vanilla and cream until smooth. Add flour and cherries. Knead and form into 2 rolls. Wrap rolls in waxed paper. Chill.

Preheat oven to 325°F. Slice dough into ¼" slices and place slices on ungreased cookie sheets. Bake for 12 minutes, or until bottoms of cookies are light golden brown.

Cool completely on wire racks and store in covered container.

Makes approximately 3 dozen cookies. These cookies freeze well.

Old—Fashioned Ginger Snaps

*Crisp ginger snaps with sugar-sparkled crackled tops
are wonderful with tea or milk.*

1 cup	butter, softened
2 cups	white sugar
2	eggs
⅞ cup	molasses
2 tsp.	baking soda
2 tsp.	water
1 tsp.	ground ginger
1 tsp.	ground cinnamon
4½ cups	all-purpose flour
	granulated sugar

Preheat oven to 375°F and lightly grease cookie sheets.

Cream butter and sugar until light. Add beaten eggs, molasses, and the baking soda which has been dissolved in the water. Blend well. Mix in spices and flour. Roll dough into balls; dip balls in granulated sugar; place on cookie sheets and flatten with the bottom of a glass dipped in flour. Bake for 8-10 minutes, or until cookies are lightly browned on the bottom.

Makes approximately 6 dozen cookies. These cookies freeze well.

Poppyseed Cookies

*These cookies were a childhood favorite of my brother.
Poppyseeds add crunchy texture and a nutty flavor.*

1 cup	butter, softened
1 cup	sugar
1	egg yolk
1½ cups	coarsely chopped hazelnuts (filberts)
½ cup	poppyseeds
½ tsp.	cinnamon
½ tsp.	ground ginger
1 tsp.	vanilla
¼ tsp.	salt
2 cups	all-purpose flour

Poppyseed Cookies
(Continued)

Cream butter and sugar until light. Add egg yolk, stir in nuts, poppyseeds, spices, vanilla and salt. Mix well. Add flour to make a firm but sticky dough. Form dough into rolls and chill.

Preheat oven to 325°F and lightly grease cookie sheets. Slice rolls into ¼" slices and place slices on cookie sheets. Bake for 10-12 minutes. Cool on wire racks.

Makes approximately 3½ dozen cookies. These cookies freeze well.

Coconut Cookies

Crisp, crunchy coconut cookies have added whole-wheat goodness.

1	**egg**
¾ cup	**butter, softened**
¾ cup	**white sugar**
½ cup	**brown sugar**
1 cup	**whole-wheat flour**
1¼ cups	**quick rolled oats**
¾ cup	**shredded coconut**
1 tsp.	**baking powder**
1 tsp.	**baking soda**

Preheat oven to 350°F and lightly grease cookie sheets.

Beat egg, add butter, brown and white sugars. Cream well. Add remaining ingredients and mix well. Drop dough by teaspoonfuls onto cookie sheets. Bake for 10-12 minutes, or until light golden brown. Cool completely.

Makes approximately 5 dozen cookies. These cookies freeze well.

13

peanut butter chip cookies

Double your satisfaction with peanut butter chips and peanut butter.

2½ cups	**sifted flour**
½ tsp.	**baking soda**
1 tsp.	**baking powder**
¼ tsp.	**salt**
1 cup	**butter, softened**
1 cup	**white sugar**
1 cup	**brown sugar**
2	**eggs**
1 cup	**peanut butter**
1 tsp.	**vanilla**
1 cup	**peanut butter chips**

Preheat oven to 375°F and lightly grease cookie sheets.

Sift together the flour, baking soda, baking powder, and salt. In a separate bowl, cream butter and sugars until light and fluffy. Add beaten eggs, peanut butter, and vanilla. Blend well. Add dry ingredients, followed by peanut butter chips. Mix thoroughly. Drop from a teaspoon 1" apart on cookie sheets. Press with a fork dipped in flour. Bake for approximately 10 minutes. Cool completely and store in a cookie tin.

Makes approximately 5 dozen cookies. These cookies freeze well.

VARIATION: Peanut butter and chocolate are a great flavor combination. Try substituting chocolate chips or chocolate chunks for the peanut chips, you'll have **Chocolate Chunk Peanut Butter Cookies.**

peanut butter

Over 100 years ago, in 1890, peanut butter was developed. It is a blend of ground peanuts, vegetable oil, salt and sometimes a bit of sugar. Peanut butter aficionados seem to be divided into two camps, creamy or chunky. Natural peanut butter, containing only peanuts and oil, can be kept for about 6 months, refrigerated.

Raisin Cookies

Soft, moist cookies with a wonderful cinnamon aroma and flavor.

2 cups	raisins
1 cup	boiling water
1 cup	butter, softened
2 cups	white sugar
3	eggs
1 tsp.	vanilla
4 cups	sifted all-purpose flour
1 tsp.	baking powder
1 tsp.	baking soda
1 tsp.	salt
1 tsp.	cinnamon
¼ tsp.	cloves
¼ tsp.	nutmeg

Preheat oven to 350°F and lightly grease cookie sheets.

Add boiling water to raisins and cook for 5 minutes; cool. Cream butter and sugar. Add eggs and vanilla and beat until fluffy. Add cooled raisins and mix thoroughly. Add flour and remaining ingredients. Blend well. Drop well-rounded teaspoonfuls of dough onto cookie sheets. Bake for 12-15 minutes, or until lightly browned. Cool cookies on wire racks. Store in a tightly covered container.

Makes approximately 5 dozen cookies. These cookies freeze well.

NOTE: To help keep cookies soft, place a quarter of an apple in the container with the cookies.

 ## Cookies

*The Dutch word **koekje** means little cake and gives us our word "cookie". The Germans have **keks**, Italians **biscotti**, English **biscuits**, Spain **galletas**. Small, crisp or soft, cakes have been popular since they were first devised in Persia in the 600s. Cookies can be **molded** or hand-formed into balls, or **pressed** into decorative shapes with a cookie press, **rolled out** and cut into shapes, rolled into logs and refrigerated (**icebox cookies**), **dropped** from a spoon onto cookie sheets, or baked in a pan and cut into **bars**.*

date pinwheel cookies

I loved these cookies as a child. My mother made them every year at Christmas time. The date filling creates a sweet chewy cookie.

¾ cup	chopped pitted dates
6 tbsp.	sugar
6 tbsp.	water
2 tsp.	lemon juice
½ tsp.	grated lemon rind
¼ cup	finely chopped pecans
⅔ cup	butter, softened
1¼ cups	firmly packed brown sugar
2 tsp.	finely grated orange rind
1	egg
1 tbsp.	vinegar
2 cups	sifted all-purpose flour
¼ tsp.	baking soda
¼ tsp.	salt

Combine dates, sugar, and water in saucepan. Cook until thickened, approximately 5 minutes, stirring constantly. Remove from heat and blend in lemon juice, lemon rind, and nuts. Cool.

Cream butter and sugar until light. Beat in orange rind, egg, and vinegar. Sift flour, baking soda and salt. Add to creamed mixture and blend well. Chill dough. Roll into a 10 x 15" rectangle. Spread with date mixture. Starting at long side, roll as for a jelly roll. Chill 1 hour.

Preheat oven to 375°F and lightly grease cookie sheets. Slice roll into ¼" slices. Place pinwheels on cookie sheets. Bake for 12-15 minutes.

Makes approximately 5 dozen cookies. These cookies freeze well.

C O O K I E S & S Q U A R E S

date nut chews

These soft chewy cookies resemble a confection.

2	eggs
¾ tsp.	salt
½ tsp.	almond extract
½ cup	sugar
½ cup	corn syrup
1 cup	chopped dates
1 cup	chopped nuts
¾ cup	sifted flour
⅓ cup	powdered (icing) sugar

Preheat oven to 375°F and lightly grease 2, 8" square layer pans.

Place eggs, salt and almond extract into a large bowl. Beat until light. Gradually beat in sugar and corn syrup. Continue beating until sugar is dissolved. Add dates and nuts and mix well. Fold in sifted flour. Pour into the greased pans. Bake for 20-30 minutes, or until a toothpick when inserted in the center comes out clean. Cut into 1½" squares and remove from pan with a knife or narrow spatula while hot. Shape into balls. Roll in powdered (icing) sugar. Cool completely and store in a tightly covered container.

Makes approximately 3 dozen cookies. These cookies freeze well.

 dates

For over 5,000 years, dates have been used in confections and desserts. Originally found in the Middle East and Africa, date palms are now grown in California and Arizona. Bursting with soft, sweet flavor, dates are available fresh or dried. They are usually oval in shape, but some are almost round. Rich in protein and iron, ripe dates range in color from golden to mahogany, brown, or black.

lemon Coconut meringue Squares

If you love lemon pie, you will love these light,
flavorful, easy-to-make squares.

Base:

½ cup	butter, softened
¼ cup	sugar
1¼ cups	all-purpose flour
1	egg yolk, beaten

Lemon Filling:

10 oz.	can (300 mL) sweetened condensed milk
2 tsp.	grated lemon rind
½ cup	lemon juice
2	egg yolks

Coconut Meringue:

3	egg whites
¼ cup	sugar
½ cup	shredded coconut
½ cup	flaked coconut

Preheat oven to 350°F and grease a 9 x 13" baking pan.

Combine butter, sugar, and flour, using a pastry blender or 2 knives, scissor fashion, until pastry resembles coarse crumbs. Stir in egg yolk and press base into prepared pan. Bake for 15 minutes, or until base is light brown. While the base is baking, combine filling ingredients in a medium bowl. Mix well. Pour over baked crust and return to oven for 10 minutes.

To make Coconut Meringue, beat egg whites in a small bowl until soft peaks form. Gradually add the ¼ cup of sugar and beat until dissolved. Fold the shredded coconut into the meringue. Spread the meringue mixture over the baked lemon filling. Sprinkle the flaked coconut over the meringue and return pan to oven for an additional 10 minutes, or until light golden brown. Remove pan from oven and cool completely. Cut into bars and store in a container in the refrigerator for up to 1 week.

Makes approximately 50 squares.

PICTURED ON PAGE 17.

almond bars

*These sweet crunchy almond and honey bars are a
classic flavor combination.*

Base:

½ cup	butter, softened
1¼ cups	all-purpose flour
¼ cup	sugar
1	egg yolk, beaten
½ tsp.	vanilla

Honey Almond Filling:

3 tbsp.	butter, softened
2 tbsp.	milk
½ cup	sugar
1½ tbsp.	honey
1 cup	blanched sliced or slivered almonds

Preheat oven to 325°F and lightly grease and flour a 9" square baking pan.

In a large bowl, cut butter into flour and sugar, using a pastry blender or 2 knives, scissor-fashion, until the mixture resembles coarse crumbs. Stir in egg yolk and vanilla. Press dough evenly into the baking pan. Bake for 10-15 minutes, or until golden brown.

In a small saucepan, heat butter, milk, sugar, honey, and almonds; stir well, until butter is melted and sauce is well blended. Spread filling over warm pastry. Return to oven and bake another 20-25 minutes, or until topping is golden brown. Cool on a rack for 10 minutes. Cut into squares or diamonds. Cool completely in pan.

Makes 3 dozen 1½" squares. These bars freeze well.

VARIATION: Try drizzling melted semisweet chocolate over cooled bars.

 almonds

The delicate, almost sweet flavor of almonds has been mentioned in the Bible, Greek and Roman writings, and also by Shakespeare. To blanch your own almonds, drop shelled almonds into boiling water for 30 seconds; drain. Cool slightly and remove the skins by rubbing the nuts between your fingers.

honeyed hazelnut bars

*The combination of orange peel and honey gives these nutty bars
an interesting flavor.*

Crust:

2½ cups	all-purpose flour
½ cup	sugar
1 cup	butter, softened
2	egg yolks

Honey Hazelnut Topping:

1 cup	butter
1 cup	honey
1 cup	brown sugar
½ cup	heavy cream
2 tbsp.	vanilla
3 tbsp.	freshly grated orange peel
3 cups	coarsely chopped toasted hazelnuts (filberts)

Preheat oven to 350°F and grease an 11 x 15" baking pan.

In a large bowl cut butter into flour and sugar, using a pastry blender or 2 knives scissor-fashion. Stir in egg yolks. Pat dough evenly in the bottom and ¼" up the sides of the prepared pan. Bake for 15-20 minutes, or until edges are lightly browned.

While base is baking prepare topping. Melt butter in a medium-sized saucepan over low heat. Stir in remaining ingredients, except nuts. Remove from heat and add nuts. Pour topping over baked crust and return to oven. Bake an additional 25 minutes, or until topping is a rich brown color. Cool for approximately 10-15 minutes and cut into bars. Let cool completely.

Makes approximately 50 bars. These bars freeze well.

peanut Crunch bars

The caramel, peanut topping creates a flavor reminiscent
of peanut brittle.

Base:

½ cup	butter, softened
½ cup	sugar
1	egg
1¼ cups	all-purpose flour
2 tbsp.	vanilla custard powder
¼ tsp.	salt

Peanut Crunch Topping:

½ cup	lightly packed brown sugar
1 tbsp.	light corn syrup
⅓ cup	butter
½ cup	coarsely chopped unsalted peanuts

Preheat oven to 350°F and lightly grease a 9" square baking pan.

Cream butter and sugar, add egg yolk and mix until fluffy. Add flour, custard powder and salt, and mix until a firm dough is formed. Press mixture into the prepared pan. Bake in oven for 15 minutes, or until light golden brown. Remove from oven

To make topping, place brown sugar, corn syrup, and butter in a small saucepan, stir over low heat until butter is melted and sugar dissolved; simmer for 5 minutes. Stir in coarsely chopped peanuts and pour over base. Return to oven for an additional 10 minutes. Remove from oven and allow to cool completely. Cut into bars and store in an airtight container.

Makes approximately 30 bars. These bars freeze well.

 Caramel

Cooked sugar caramelizes when it melts, about 320-350°F on a candy thermometer, and becomes a thick, clear golden-brown liquid. Cooled caramel hardens and can easily be cracked, for nut brittles, or crushed to be used as a topping for ice cream. Sugar and water can be cooked together, about 1 cup of sugar to ¼ cup of water, in a heavy saucepan to form a thinner caramel syrup.

Orange Matrimonial bars

The orange gives these bars their zesty flavor,
a delightful change from traditional matrimonial bars.
This was a favorite of one of our best customers.

Pecan Oat Base:

1½ cups	all-purpose flour
1 tsp.	baking soda
1 tsp.	salt
½ cup	chopped pecans
2½ cups	rolled oats
1½ cups	firmly packed brown sugar
1 cup	butter, melted

Orange Date Filling:

1 lb.	pitted dates, chopped
½ cup	granulated sugar
¾ cup	light corn syrup
¼ cup	orange juice
1 tbsp.	fresh grated orange rind
¼ tsp.	salt

Preheat oven to 350°F and lightly grease a 9 x 13" pan.

Combine base ingredients. Press half of dough firmly into prepared pan. Reserve remaining dough and make filling.

Combine filling ingredients in a large saucepan, simmer over medium heat until the mixture is thick. Pour filling over base and cover with reserved dough. Pat down dough firmly. Bake for 25-35 minutes, or until golden brown. Remove pan from oven and let cool. Cut into bars.

Makes approximately 36 bars. These bars freeze well.

VARIATION: If you prefer the traditional version, omit the orange rind and juice and add 2 tbsp. EACH lemon juice and water, plus ½ tsp. vanilla.

Coffee Streusel Bars

Cappuccino-flavored bars with a rich coffee-cake-like topping.

Cinnamon Brown Sugar Topping:

1 cup	all-purpose flour
2 tsp.	cinnamon
⅓ cup	firmly packed brown sugar
½ cup	butter, softened

Base:

½ cup	butter, softened
¼ cup	sugar
1¼ cups	all-purpose flour
1	egg yolk, beaten

Coffee Pecan Filling:

10 oz.	can (300 mL) sweetened condensed milk
2 tbsp.	butter
2 tbsp.	corn syrup
3 tsp.	instant coffee powder
⅓ cup	finely chopped pecans

To make the topping, combine flour, cinnamon, brown sugar, and butter, mixing until a firm dough is formed. Refrigerate for ½ hour.

Preheat oven to 350°F and lightly grease a 9 x 13" baking pan.

To make the base, combine flour and sugar in a medium-sized bowl. Cut in butter into flour mixture, using a pastry blender or 2 knives, scissor fashion, until mixture resembles coarse crumbs. Mix in egg yolk. Press dough into prepared pan. Bake for 10 minutes, or until light golden brown.

Meanwhile, to make the filling, combine first 4 ingredients in a saucepan and cook over medium heat, stirring constantly until mixture comes to a soft boil. Continue to cook, stirring constantly for an additional 5 minutes, until thick. Remove from heat and spread filling evenly over hot base. Allow to cool for about 10 minutes, then use a coarse grater to grate topping dough evenly over filling.

Return pan to oven and bake for an additional 10-15, minutes, or until the topping is firm to the touch. Remove from the oven and cool completely. Cut into bars.

Makes approximately 36 bars. These freeze well.

Triple Chocolate Cookie Bars

Chocolate, chocolate, chocolate, what more can we say!

½ cup	butter
1⅓ cups	graham cracker crumbs
½ cup	semisweet chocolate chips
½ cup	milk chocolate chips
½ cup	white chocolate chips
½ cup	flaked coconut
1 cup	chopped pecans
10 oz.	can (300 mL) sweetened condensed milk

Preheat oven to 350°F and grease a 9 x 13" pan.

Melt butter and add graham crumbs. Press into prepared pan. Sprinkle chocolate chips over the crumbs, followed by the coconut and the chopped nuts. Pour the sweetened condensed milk evenly over the other ingredients. Bake for 25-30 minutes, or until lightly browned. Cool and cut into bars. Store in a sealed container.

Makes approximately 36 bars. These bars freeze well.

Milk Chocolate-Glazed Brownies

*Grandma Derheim, my husband's grandmother, made these moist,
rich double-chocolate brownies.*

⅔ cup	butter, softened
1 cup	sugar
2	eggs, beaten
1 tsp.	vanilla
1 cup	flour
½ tsp.	salt
5 tbsp.	unsweetened cocoa
½ cup	chopped nuts
8 oz.	milk chocolate, melted

milk chocolate–glazed brownies
(Continued)

Preheat oven to 325°F and grease an 8 or 9" square pan. Set aside.

Cream butter and sugar together until light. Stir in beaten eggs. Blend well. Add remaining ingredients, except milk chocolate. Mix thoroughly. Pour batter into prepared pan. Bake for 20 minutes, or until just set in the middle. Do not overbake, brownies should be moist inside. When brownies are cool, pour melted chocolate over top and let set. Brownies will be easier to cut if the chocolate is scored with a sharp knife just before it is completely set. When completely cool cut into squares. Store in a sealed container in the refrigerator.

Makes approximately 36 bars. These freeze well.

Caramel pecan bars

Base:

1 cup	butter, softened
2½ cups	all-purpose flour
½ cup	white sugar
2	egg yolks, beaten

Caramel Pecan Filling:

4 cups	pecan halves
¾ cup	butter
½ cup	liquid honey
¾ cup	lightly packed brown sugar
¼ cup	whipping cream

Preheat oven to 325°F and lightly grease a 10 x 15" baking pan.

In a large bowl, cut butter into flour and sugar using a pastry blender or 2 knives, scissor-fashion, until mixture resembles coarse crumbs. Stir in egg yolks. Press dough into prepared pan and bake for 10-15 minutes, or until golden.

Spread pecans evenly over baked crust. In a large heavy saucepan melt butter and honey. Add brown sugar. Boil 5-7 minutes stirring constantly, until a rich caramel color. Remove from heat. Stir in cream; mix well and pour over pecans. Bake 15 minutes, or until set. Cool and cut into bars.

Makes approximately 50 bars. These freeze well.

PICTURED ON PAGE 17.

27

Chocolate-Coated Toffee bars

Crust:

2½ cups	all-purpose flour
1 cup	butter, softened
½ cup	white sugar
1	egg yolk

Toffee Filling:

10 oz.	can (300 mL) sweetened condensed milk
¼ cup	corn syrup
1 cup	butter
1 cup	brown sugar

Topping:

12 oz.	semisweet chocolate

Preheat oven to 325°F and lightly grease a 10 x 15" baking pan or 2, 9" square baking pans.

Combine flour, butter, and sugar, using a pastry blender or 2 knives, scissor-fashion, until pastry resembles coarse crumbs. Stir in egg yolk and press dough evenly into prepared pan(s). Bake for 15-20 minutes, or until lightly browned.

In a heavy saucepan, combine condensed milk, syrup, butter, and brown sugar. Stir over medium heat and bring to a gentle boil. Let boil for a full 5 minutes while stirring constantly. Remove from heat and spread over baked crust. Let cool completely.

Melt semisweet chocolate. Pour over cooled filling and spread evenly. Cool until chocolate is almost set. Score into bars using a sharp knife. When chocolate is completely set, finish cutting bars and remove from pan. Store in refrigerator in a sealed container.

Makes approximately 50 bars.

Cakes & Tortes

Grand Marnier Cake

A light moist cake with a hint of orange.

Cookie Base:

3 tbsp.	butter, softened
⅓ cup	sugar
¾ cup	flour
1	egg

White Cake:

4	eggs, separated
¼ cup	warm water
1 tsp.	vanilla
¾ cup	sugar
1½ cups	sifted cake flour
1½ tsp.	baking powder
½ tsp.	baking soda

Grand Marnier Syrup:

⅓ cup	sugar
½ cup	water
¼ cup	Grand Marnier OR other orange-flavored liqueur

Grand Marnier Whipped Cream Frosting:

3 tsp.	unflavored gelatin
¼ cup	water
3 cups	whipping cream
½ cup	powdered sugar
1 tbsp.	undiluted frozen concentrated orange juice
1 tbsp.	Grand Marnier
	candied orange slices for garnish

Preheat oven to 325°F. Grease 3, 9" cake pans and line with waxed paper or parchment circles.

To make the cookie base, combine butter, sugar, flour, and egg; press base mixture into the bottom of 1 of the cake pans. Bake base for 10-12 minutes, or until it begins to turn light brown. Remove from the oven, allow to cool in the pan for 10 minutes, then remove from pan and allow to cool completely on a wire rack.

Grand Marnier Cake
(Continued)

To make the cake, in a medium bowl, beat egg yolks and water until foamy. Add vanilla and sugar, and beat until thick and pale. In another bowl, sift together cake flour, baking powder, and baking soda. Gradually sift and fold dry ingredients into egg yolk mixture. In a third bowl beat egg whites until stiff but not dry. Fold beaten egg whites into batter. Pour batter into 2 prepared pans. Bake for 20-25 minutes, or until a toothpick inserted in the middle comes out clean. Cool cakes in pans for 10 minutes then transfer cakes to wire racks to cool completely.

To make the syrup, in a small saucepan, combine sugar and water. Bring to a boil over medium heat, stirring until sugar is dissolved. Boil for 3 minutes. Remove from heat and add Grand Marnier. Cool completely.

To make frosting, sprinkle gelatin over cold water in a small saucepan. Let stand for 3 minutes. Place over low heat, stirring constantly until the gelatin dissolves. Remove from heat and cool slightly. In a large bowl whip cream and sugar until cream starts to thicken. Slowly add cooled gelatin to cream mixture while beating on high speed. Next add the orange juice and Grand Marnier. Beat mixture until soft peaks form and whipping cream is stiff enough to spread.

To assemble cake, place base cookie layer on a flat cake plate. Spread ¼ of the whipped cream mixture on the cookie. Next, place a sponge cake layer on top of whipping cream. Spray top of the sponge generously with syrup mixture.* Sponge should be moist but not soggy.** Spread whipping cream on top of the second layer. Top with the third layer and spray sponge with syrup. Spread whipping cream on top and sides of cake, reserving some whipped cream for garnish. Using a pastry bag with a star tip attachment, make rosettes around the top outside edge of the cake. Garnish with candied orange slices. Refrigerate until serving.

* Spray bottles used for misting plants work well for this and are relatively inexpensive.

** When working with sponge cake, the key to keeping the cake moist is to spray with a syrup mixture; this does not mean that the cake has to be soggy.

Serves 10-12.

Chocolate Cinnamon Torte

Cinnamon Cookies:

2 cups	sugar
1⅔ cups	butter, softened
2	eggs
2 tbsp.	cinnamon
2¾ cups	all-purpose flour

Chocolate Cream Filling:

4 cups	whipping cream
½ cup	unsweetened cocoa
¼ cup	powdered (icing) sugar

Topping and Garnish:

6 oz.	milk chocolate, coarsely grated
4 oz.	semisweet chocolate

Preheat oven to 375°F. Cut out 14, 9" circles from waxed or parchment paper and set aside.

To make cookies, into a large bowl, measure sugar, butter, eggs, cinnamon, and flour. Beat on high speed until dough resembles soft whipping cream. Place parchment circles on cookie sheets and, with a metal spatula, spread ⅓ cup of dough evenly over each circle. Bake 8-12 minutes, or until lightly browned around edges. Carefully remove cookies, still on waxed paper, from cookie sheet to cooling rack. Cool completely. Repeat until all dough is used. Stack cooled cookies on a flat plate, cover with plastic wrap and store in a cool dry place. **The cookies can be made several days ahead.**

To make filling, early in the day or one day ahead, in a large bowl beat cream, cocoa, and powdered sugar on high until soft peaks form. Carefully peel off waxed paper from 1 cookie. Place cookie on a flat cake plate. Spread first cookie with ½ cup of whipped cream mixture. Repeat layering until all cookies are used, ending with cream on top. Pile grated milk chocolate on top of the cake. Refrigerate the cake until serving, a minimum of 3 hours, to allow the cookies to soften.

At least 1 hour before serving, melt semisweet chocolate and spread over a 9" round parchment circle. When chocolate just starts to set, score circle into 16 wedges. Allow chocolate to harden in refrigerator. Break chocolate into wedges and use to garnish torte. Cut and serve.

Serves 16.

Strawberry Almond Shortcake

A wonderful almond-flavored shortcake, perfect for summer celebrations.

Almond Shortbread Cookies:

2 cups	ground almonds
1½ cups	sifted cake flour
1 cup	butter, softened
1¼ cups	sugar
3	egg yolks
¼ tsp.	almond extract

Amaretto Whipped Cream Filling:

2½ cups	whipping cream
⅓ cup	sugar
2 tbsp.	amaretto OR ¼ tsp. almond extract
1 tsp.	vanilla
3 cups	sliced fresh strawberries
	whole strawberries for garnish
	melted chocolate for garnish (optional)

Preheat oven to 350°F. Cut 4, 9" round circles from parchment or waxed paper.

To make the cookies, combine cookie ingredients and mix until a soft dough is formed. Divide dough into four and spread evenly on each of the parchment circles, placed on a baking sheet. Bake for 15 minutes, or until lightly browned. Remove cookies from oven and cool on wire racks.

To make the filling, beat the whipping cream until soft peaks form. Gradually add the sugar, amaretto, and vanilla. Peel the waxed paper from one of the cookies and place it on a flat cake plate. Spread ¼ of the whipping cream mixture on the first cookie followed by ¼ of the sliced strawberries. Top with second cookie. Continue the process until all the cookies, cream and strawberries are used, ending with cream and strawberries on top. Refrigerate for a minimum of 1 hour. Garnish with whole strawberries and drizzle with melted chocolate, if you wish. Cut and serve.

Serves 8-10.

PICTURED ON THE FRONT COVER.

Almond Date Carrot Cake

Apples and dates make this cake very moist and flavorful.
This carrot cake was often requested as a wedding cake.

Almond Date Carrot Cake:

1½ cups	sugar
1½ cups	vegetable oil
3	eggs
2 tsp.	vanilla
2 cups	sifted all-purpose flour
2 tsp.	cinnamon
1 tsp.	baking powder
1 tsp.	baking soda
1 tsp.	salt
2 cups	shredded carrots
1 cup	coarsely chopped apples
1 cup	chopped dates
1 cup	slivered almonds

Cinnamon Cream Cheese Frosting:

1 cup	softened butter
8 oz.	softened cream cheese
3 cups	powdered sugar
1½ tsp.	cinnamon
2 tbsp.	milk

Preheat oven to 350°F. Grease 2, 9" round cake pans and line the bottoms with waxed paper or parchment circles. Set pans aside.

Combine sugar, oil, eggs and vanilla in a large bowl; blend thoroughly. Sift together dry ingredients; add to the oil mixture and mix well. Stir in carrots, apples, dates, and almonds. Pour batter into prepared pans. Bake for 35-45 minutes, or until the center of the cake is firm to the touch. Cool in the pans for 10 minutes. Remove from pans and finish cooling on wire racks.

While cake is cooling make the frosting. Cream the butter and cream cheese together until smooth. Add the powdered sugar, cinnamon, and milk. Mix until smooth. Fill and frost the cooled cake.

Store the cake in the refrigerator.

Serves 10-12.

 34

CAKES & CONFECTIONS

Luscious Lemon Cake, page 38
White Chocolate Truffles, page 80
Milk Chocolate Truffles, page 83
Brandy, Amaretto & Rum Truffles, page 82

lemon Sour Cream pound Cake

This is a moist buttery pound cake, excellent as a snack cake or a good base cake for decorating. We used this recipe a lot for wedding cakes. The flavors mature after 1 or 2 days, but the cake is more moist when fresh.

1¼ cups	butter, softened
3 cups	sugar
7	eggs
2 tsp.	grated fresh lemon rind OR zest
1 tsp.	vanilla
3½ cups	sifted cake and pastry flour
½ tsp.	baking soda
1¼ cups	sour cream

Preheat oven to 350°F. Grease 2, 3 x 5 x 9" loaf pans* and set aside.

Cream butter and sugar together in a large bowl. Add eggs, one at a time, beating after each addition. Beat in lemon rind and vanilla. Combine dry ingredients and add to egg mixture in 3 parts alternating with the sour cream. Mix thoroughly after each addition. Pour batter into prepared pans. Bake for 45-55 minutes, or until a toothpick comes out clean when inserted in center of cake. Cool in pans for 10 minutes then turn onto a wire cooling rack. Cool completely, slice and serve.

Serves 10-12. This cake freezes well.

* This cake may also be baked in 2, 9" round cake pans and frosted, if desired, or a large bundt pan may be used.

VARIATION: *For* **Chocolate Pound Cake** *substitute ¼ cup of unsweetened cocoa for the lemon rind and reduce flour to 3¼ cups.*

 ## lemons

Zesty and refreshing, lemons originated in Southeastern Asia. Grate lemon peel before juicing the lemon. Use a zester, vegetable peeler, or a fine grater. One lemon yields 1-2 tsp. of peel. The zest is the fragrant, colored part of the peel that is full of aromatic oil. To freeze grated peel, spread it on a cookie sheet and freeze it, uncovered. Quickly place the frozen peel in plastic bags and refreeze.

luscious lemon Cake

White Cake:

4	eggs, separated
¼ cup	warm water
1 tsp.	vanilla
¾ cup	sugar
1½ cups	sifted cake flour
1½ tsp.	baking powder
½ tsp.	baking soda

Lemon Filling:

¾ cup	sugar
½ cup	fresh lemon juice
2	whole eggs
3	egg yolks
1 tbsp.	freshly grated lemon peel
6 tbsp.	butter, softened

Grand Marnier Syrup:

½ cup	water
⅓ cup	sugar
¼ cup	Grand Marnier

Lemon Whipped Cream Frosting:

1 tbsp.	unflavored gelatin (1 envelope)
¼ cup	water
3 cups	whipping cream
½ cup	powdered sugar
1½ tsp.	finely grated lemon peel
	candied lemon pieces OR peel for garnish

Preheat oven to 325°F. Grease and flour 3, 9" round cake pans.

To make the cake, in a large bowl, beat egg yolks and water until foamy. Add vanilla and sugar, beat until thick and pale. In a medium bowl, sift together cake flour, baking powder, and baking soda. Slowly sift dry ingredients into egg yolk mixture. Stir until blended.

In a third bowl, beat egg whites until stiff but not dry. Fold beaten egg whites into batter. Pour into the prepared cake pans. Bake for 20 minutes, or until a toothpick comes out clean when inserted. Cool cakes in pans for 10 minutes then turn out onto wire racks to cool completely.

luscious lemon Cake

(Continued)

To make the filling, in the top of a double boiler, beat together all the ingredients, except the butter. Cook over simmering water until the mixture thickens. Next, gradually beat in butter, adding 1 tbsp. at a time. Transfer filling to a glass bowl; cover. Filling can also be made in the microwave. Microwave on medium, beating mixture every 1½ minutes. This will take 5-7 minutes. Remove from microwave and add the butter. Place filling in refrigerator to chill.

To make the syrup, in a small saucepan, combine sugar and water. Bring to a boil over medium heat, stirring until sugar is completely dissolved. Boil for additional 3 minutes. Remove from heat and add Grand Marnier. Cool.

To make the frosting, sprinkle gelatin over water in a small saucepan, let stand for 3 minutes. Stir mixture over low heat until gelatin dissolves, then set aside to cool.* In a 5-quart bowl, combine whipping cream and powdered sugar. Beat until mixture just starts to thicken, slowly add the gelatin to the whipping cream mixture and beat at high speed until stiff peaks form. Gently fold the grated lemon peel into the whipped cream mixture.

To assemble the cake, place the first layer on a flat cake plate. Spray with ⅓ of Grand Marnier mixture. (See note on page 31.) Fill a pastry bag with the whipped cream mixture and pipe a ring around the top edge of the first cake layer. Spread ½ the filling inside the ring. Place the second layer on top of the first and repeat the procedure. Top with the third cake layer; spray the sponge, and spread whipping cream on sides and top of the cake. If desired, use the piping bag and part of the remaining whipping cream to create rosettes on top of the cake. Garnish with candied lemon pieces. Refrigerate until served.

Serves 10-12.

* Gelatin should be warm but not hot to the touch. Do not allow it to set.

PICTURED ON PAGE 35.

Tiramisu Cake

This is a very rich and moist, amaretto-flavored cake. It is my
variation on the traditional Tiramisu with lady fingers.

Vanilla Sponge Cake:

4	eggs, separated
¼ cup	warm water
1 tsp.	vanilla
¾ cup	sugar
1½ cups	sifted cake flour
1½ tsp.	baking powder
½ tsp.	baking soda

Coffee Amaretto Syrup:

1¼ cups	water
⅞ cup	sugar
1½ tsp.	powdered instant coffee
3 tbsp.	amaretto

Amaretto Filling:

1 tbsp.	unflavored gelatin (1 envelope)
¼ cup	water
8 oz.	softened cream cheese
3 tbsp.	amaretto
3 cups	whipping cream
½ cup	powdered sugar

Topping:

¼ cup	cocoa

Preheat oven to 350°F. Grease 2, 9" round cake pans and line with waxed paper or parchment circles.

In a medium bowl, beat egg yolks and water until foamy. Add vanilla and sugar, beat until thick and pale. Into another bowl, sift together cake flour, baking powder, and baking soda. Gradually sift dry ingredients into egg yolk mixture. Blend well. In a medium bowl, beat egg whites until stiff but not dry. Fold beaten egg whites into batter. Pour batter into prepared pans. Bake for 20-25 minutes, or until a toothpick inserted in middle comes out clean. Cool cakes for 10 minutes in pans then remove from pans and cool completely on wire racks.

Tiramisu Cake

(Continued)

While cakes are cooling make filling and syrup.

To make syrup, bring water and sugar to a boil, add coffee powder and amaretto and remove syrup from heat. Allow syrup to cool completely.

To make filling, sprinkle gelatin over water in a small saucepan. Let stand 3 minutes. Place over low heat, stirring constantly, until the gelatin dissolves. Remove from heat and cool until just warm to the touch.

Beat cream cheese and amaretto together until smooth. Set aside. Whip cream and sugar together until it begins to thicken. While beating slowly, gradually add cooled gelatin to whipped cream mixture. Whip at high speed until stiff. Gradually add the whipping cream mixture to the cream cheese mixture. Beat until smooth.

To assemble, lightly soak the top of the bottom layer of sponge cake, on the top side only, with ½ of the cooled syrup. Spread ⅓ of whipped cream filling on top of the first sponge. Next, soak the second sponge layer on both sides with the remaining syrup. Place the second layer on top of first. Spread remaining whipped cream on top and sides of cake.

Sift cocoa on top of the cake. Refrigerate until serving.

Serves 10-12.

 # Tiramisu

The name of this very popular Italian cake means "lift me up". The traditional version uses mascarpone cheese, a double cream dessert cheese which is buttery and rich, but also very expensive. It can be difficult to find unless you live in a large city. To substitute for mascarpone, beat together ½ cream cheese and ½ ricotta cheese OR beat together 1 cup (8 oz.) of softened cream cheese and 1 tbsp. of butter, plus ¼ cup of sour cream.

rich Turtle Chocolate Cake

A very moist chocolate cake with a rich turtle-like filling. A big hit with both the big and little children in my family.

Sour Cream Chocolate Cake:

1¼ cups	sifted flour
1 tsp.	baking soda
¼ cup	unsweetened cocoa
2	eggs
1 cup	brown sugar
1 tsp.	vanilla
1 cup	sour cream
¼ tsp.	salt
¼ cup	boiling water

Caramel Pecan Filling:

½ x 10 oz.	can (300 mL) sweetened condensed milk
2 tbsp.	corn syrup
½ cup	butter
½ cup	brown sugar
1 cup	chopped pecans

Chocolate Butter Icing*:

¾ cup	butter, softened
2 cups	powdered sugar
¼ cup	unsweetened cocoa
2 tbsp.	milk

Preheat oven to 350°F. Grease and flour 2, 9" round cake pans. Line bottom of pans with waxed paper or parchment circles.

To make the cake, combine flour, baking soda, and cocoa. Beat eggs well and add brown sugar. Beat until light. Add vanilla, sour cream, and salt and blend well. Add flour mixture. Blend well. Stir in the boiling water and pour into prepared pans. Bake for 20-25 minutes, or until a toothpick comes out clean when inserted in the center of the cake. Remove from oven and cool in pans for 15 minutes. Remove cakes from pans and cool completely on wire racks.

rich Turtle Chocolate Cake
(Continued)

To make the filling, in a heavy saucepan, combine condensed milk, syrup, butter, and brown sugar. Stir over medium heat and bring to a gentle boil. Allow to boil for a full 5 minutes, stirring constantly. Remove from heat and stir in chopped pecans. Allow to cool completely.

Meanwhile, prepare icing. Combine softened butter, sugar, cocoa, and milk. Beat until light and fluffy. Place one of the cooled cakes on a flat cake plate. Top with caramel filling. Top with the second cake layer and spread the icing on sides and top of cake.

Serves 8-10.

* For a less sweet cake, try icing it with whipped cream.

brown Sugar Crumb Cake

A great cake for snacks or afternoon coffee. I don't know if this cake freezes well or not, because it is always eaten the day it is baked.

1½ cups	brown sugar
2 cups	sifted all-purpose flour
2 tsp.	baking powder
1 cup	butter, softened
2	eggs, well beaten
¾ cup	milk
½ tsp.	vanilla

Preheat oven to 350°F and lightly grease a, 9" square cake pan.

In a large bowl, mix brown sugar, flour, baking powder, and butter together until crumbly. Take ¾ cup of the flour mixture and set it aside. To the remainder add well-beaten eggs, milk, and vanilla. Pour the batter into the prepared cake pan and cover with the reserved crumb mixture. Bake for 30-35 minutes, or until a toothpick inserted in the center of the cake comes out clean. Remove the cake from the oven and cool completely in the pan before cutting.

Serves 12.

Chocolate Almond Brownie Cake

A very rich treat for 16 of your favorite people.

Chocolate Almond Brownie:

12 oz.	semisweet chocolate (12 squares)
2 cups	butter, softened
2½ cups	sugar
7	eggs, separated
1 tsp.	almond extract
2⅓ cups	ground almonds
1 cup	all-purpose flour

White Chocolate Ganache Soufflé:

8 oz.	white chocolate (8 squares)
1 cup	whipping cream

Chocolate Glaze:

½ cup	butter
8 oz.	semisweet chocolate (8 squares)
4 tbsp.	whipping cream

Chocolate Curls:

6 oz.	semisweet chocolate (6 squares)

Preheat oven to 350°F. Grease and flour 3, 9" round cake pans; line with waxed or parchment paper and set aside.

To make the cake, melt semisweet chocolate in a bowl over simmering water or in a double boiler. Allow the chocolate to cool slightly. In a large bowl, cream butter and sugar until light. Add the egg yolks, 1 at a time, beating well after each addition. Stir in the melted chocolate. Add the almond extract, followed by the ground almonds and flour; stir just until the mixture is blended. In a separate medium bowl, beat egg whites until soft peaks form. Gently fold beaten egg whites into the chocolate brownie mixture. Pour batter into prepared pans and bake for 20-25 minutes, or until the cakes are just set. The cakes should be quite moist. Do NOT overbake! Remove cakes from the oven and allow to cool in pans for 15 minutes. Gently remove cakes from pans and finish cooling on a wire rack. If not assembling the cake until later, be sure to wrap the layers well to avoid drying.

Chocolate Almond Brownie Cake

(Continued)

To make the ganache, break white chocolate into small pieces. Pour the whipping cream into a medium pot and add chocolate pieces. Heat mixture over low heat until chocolate is completely melted. Stir constantly to keep chocolate from burning. Set chocolate mixture in refrigerator and allow to cool completely. When cool (not cold) to the touch, whip chocolate mixture with a small beater until it is of spreading consistency. The mixture will change from a creamy yellow color to almost white. As soon as this occurs quickly spread a small amount on 1 cake layer. Top with the second layer add more ganache. Top with the third layer and, as quickly as possible, spread remaining ganache on sides and top of cake. Place the cake in the refrigerator to allow ganache to completely harden and cool, approximately 15-20 minutes.

Make the glaze while the cake is cooling. Heat butter and semisweet chocolate in a double boiler over low heat; add cream and mix well. Allow glaze to cool slightly so that it is cool (not cold) to the touch. Pour glaze over the cooled cake and return it to the refrigerator to set. When glaze is nearly dry, garnish the top of the cake with chocolate curls.

Chocolate Curls: To make chocolate curls, melt 6 oz. of semisweet chocolate over low heat and spread over a piece of parchment paper. The chocolate should be no thinner than ¼". Allow chocolate to set in the refrigerator. When chocolate is completely set but slightly pliable it is ready. To create curls, pull either a cheese slicer or a carrot peeler across the chocolate at about a 45 degree angle. Try to handle curls as little as possible. The chocolate curls can be made ahead of time and kept in the refrigerator until needed.

For greater ease when slicing the cake, warm the serving knife before cutting.

Serves 16.

dark Chocolate mocha Cake

A dark luscious chocolate cake with a hint of coffee.
Mocha Buttercream is a little more time consuming than the usual
buttercream, but the finished result is well worth the effort.

Chocolate Mocha Cake:

1 cup	boiling water
4 oz.	unsweetened chocolate (4 squares)
¾ cup	butter, softened
2 cups	sugar
2	eggs, separated
1 tsp.	vanilla
2 tbsp.	Kahlúa
2 cups	all-purpose flour
1 tsp.	baking soda
1½ tsp.	baking powder
½ cup	buttermilk

Mocha Buttercream Frosting:

4	egg yolks, beaten
½ cup	sugar
1 cup	milk
1 tbsp.	cornstarch
2 tbsp.	unsweetened cocoa
2 tbsp.	Kahlúa
¾ cup	butter, softened
¾ cup	powdered sugar

Preheat oven to 350°F. Grease and flour 2, 9" round cake pans. Set aside.

To make the cake, pour boiling water over unsweetened chocolate in a small bowl and stir to melt chocolate. Let cool. Cream butter and sugar until fluffy. Add egg yolks 1 at a time, blending well after each addition. Add melted chocolate, vanilla, and Kahlúa to butter mixture; blend well. Sift together flour, baking soda, and baking powder. Add flour to chocolate mixture alternately with buttermilk. In a separate bowl, beat egg whites until soft peaks form. Gently fold egg whites into batter and pour into prepared pan. Bake for 25-30 minutes, or until a toothpick inserted in the center comes out clean. Remove from oven and cool in pans for 10 minutes. Remove cake layers from pans; cool completely on wire racks.

dark Chocolate Mocha Cake
(Continued)

To prepare frosting, in a medium bowl combine egg yolks, sugar, milk, cornstarch, cocoa, and Kahlúa. Beat well. Microwave on medium for 7-8 minutes, or until mixture thickens. Be sure to beat mixture every 1½ minutes. Cool completely in the refrigerator. Beat butter and powdered sugar together. Add 1 spoonful at a time to cooled egg mixture and beat until light. Spread frosting between layers and over cake. Store in refrigerator.

Serves 8-10.

Chocolate-dipped Fruits

Delicious and decorative, chocolate-coated fruit can be a treat on its own or used as a beautiful garnish. These are best eaten the same day they are made, except for the dried apricots which will keep for several days.

semisweet or sweet chocolate

assorted fruit:
  strawberries
  orange OR tangerine sections
  dried apricots
  cherries
  grapes
  raspberries
  apple OR pear slices
  bananas

Make sure that the fruit is clean and dry. Leave stems on whole fruits.

In a small deep saucepan, melt chocolate over very low heat. Remove from the heat. Or use a small deep bowl and melt chocolate in the microwave. Using the fruit stem or a toothpick, dip the fruit into the chocolate; wipe excess chocolate off against pan edge; place coated fruit on waxed paper to set. Refrigerate for faster setting. Reheat chocolate when it becomes too thick. Strawberries and other whole fruit may be dipped halfway; with sliced fruit, dip the entire piece of fruit.

PICTURED ON THE FRONT COVER.

black forest cake

The original version of this famous cake comes from the Black Forest region in Germany. Spraying the cake with a fine mist of Kirsch Syrup is the secret to keeping this cake moist, and sour cherries heighten the flavor. Kirsch lovers often add it to the whipped cream frosting as well as the cake.

Chocolate Cake:

4	eggs, separated
¼ cup	warm water
¾ cup	sugar
1 tsp.	vanilla
1¼ cups	sifted cake flour
¼ cup	unsweetened cocoa
2 tsp.	baking powder
½ tsp.	baking soda

Kirsch Syrup:

⅓ cup	sugar
½ cup	water
¼ cup	kirsch

Sour Cherry Filling:

⅓ cup	sugar
2 tbsp.	cornstarch
28 oz.	can (796 mL) sour pitted cherries

Whipped Cream Frosting:

4 tsp.	unflavored gelatin**
⅓ cup	water
4 cups	whipping cream
½ cup	powdered sugar
6 oz.	semisweet chocolate

Preheat oven to 375°F. Grease, flour, and line with parchment circles 3, 9" round cake pans. Set aside.

To make the cake, in a large bowl, beat egg yolks and water until foamy. Add the sugar and vanilla; beat until pale and thick. Combine cake flour, cocoa, baking powder, and baking soda. Gradually fold dry ingredients into egg yolk mixture. Beat egg whites until stiff but not dry; fold egg whites into batter. Pour batter into prepared pans. Bake for 20-25 minutes, or until a toothpick comes out clean when inserted in center of the cake.

black forest cake
(Continued)

Remove pans from the oven and immediately run a knife around the cakes, between sides of pan and cake. Cool in pans for 10 minutes then remove from pans and finish cooling on a wire cooling rack. When cool, cover cakes to keep them from drying out.

To make syrup, in a small saucepan combine water and sugar. Stir over medium heat until sugar dissolves. Bring to a rolling boil. Remove from heat and add kirsch. Cool syrup completely and put into a spray bottle. Unused plant spray bottles work well. If a spray bottle is not available, syrup can be "painted" on the cake layers with a pastry or basting brush.

Make the filling while the syrup cools. In a medium saucepan combine sugar, cornstarch, and cherries. Stir over medium heat until mixture thickens. (Cherries can also be microwaved on medium until thick. Make sure to stir every minute and a half.) Cool filling to room temperature.

To make frosting, sprinkle gelatin over water in a small saucepan, let stand for 3 minutes. Stir over low heat until gelatin** dissolves; set aside to cool. In a large bowl whip cream and sugar until cream starts to thicken. Slowly add cooled gelatin to cream while beating on high speed. Beat until stiff peaks form.

To assemble a Black Forest Cake*:
An easy way to assemble a Black Forest cake, that ensures an even finish, is to use a ring mold or ring from a cheesecake pan. You will need a ring that is slightly larger than the size of your sponge cake, e.g., if the sponge is 9", use a 9½-10" ring. Place the first layer of sponge cake on a flat cake plate or pan that is at least 2" larger than the sponge. Fill a pastry bag with part of the whipped cream mixture**. Place the ring around the sponge cake. There should be space between the sides of the ring and the sponge. Next, spray the sponge layer with the kirsch syrup mixture. Pipe whipping cream around the cake, filling in the gap between the ring and the cake. Pipe a circle around the outer edge of the cake as well as one in the center.

Continued on the next page.

black Forest Cake
(Continued)

These circles will help keep the filling from oozing out over the edge of the cake. Place half of the cherry filling inside the whipped cream circles. Top filling with second sponge layer and repeat the process. Top with the third sponge layer and spray sponge lightly with syrup. If sponge is higher than the top of the ring don't be afraid to push it down slightly. Cover the top of cake with whipping cream. Using a large metal spatula or flat knife, level whipping cream so it is even with the top of the metal ring. Place the cake in the refrigerator or freezer to set, for at least half an hour. When set, remove metal ring by running a knife around edge and lifting off. Smooth any rough edges and garnish cake with remainder of whipped cream. Grated chocolate can be applied to sides of the cake with a flat plastic scraper. Scoop some of the shavings onto the scraper and hold the tip of the scraper against the bottom of the cake at about a 45° angle. Quickly and lightly push the scrapper against the side of the cake. Chocolate should adhere to sides. Repeat process around entire cake. Clean excess chocolate and cream off the sides of the cake plate. Chill and serve.

Serves 12.

* This method may also be used for assembling other tortes or cakes that have sponge bases and whipped cream frosting.

** It is necessary to use stabilized whipped cream (whipped cream with gelatin or stabilizer added to it) for this method as it will allow the whipped cream to hold its shape and keep it from turning watery.

PICTURED ON THE BACK COVER.

Coconut Christmas Cake

Almonds and coconut add lovely flavor and texture to this unusual Christmas cake.

½ cup	butter, softened
2 cups	sugar
6	eggs
1 cup	milk
1 tsp.	vanilla
2 tsp.	almond extract
2 cups	all-purpose flour
1 lb.	raisins
1 lb.	coconut
¼ lb.	citron peel
1 lb.	blanched slivered almonds
½ lb.	glazed cherries

Preheat oven to 275°F. Grease 2, 4½ x 8" loaf pans and line with greased parchment paper.

Cream butter and sugar together. Add beaten eggs followed by milk. Add vanilla and almond extracts. Sift flour and add to egg mixture, blending well. Add remaining ingredients, stirring well. Pour into prepared pans. Bake 2 hours, or until a toothpick inserted in the middle comes out clean. Cool in pans for 10 minutes then turn onto wire racks to cool completely. Wrap cakes well and store in the refrigerator or freezer.

Makes approximately 4 pounds of cake.

 # Fruitcakes

These traditional holiday cakes have been made in many countries. Heavy with candied fruit, peel, spices, and nuts, and liberally splashed with brandy or other liquors, they are often more fruit than cake. Molasses or brown sugar and dark-colored fruits, such as prunes, dates, and raisins are used in dark fruitcakes. Light fruitcakes use corn syrup or sugar and light-colored fruit such as golden raisins, dried apricots, citron peel, plus almonds. Well wrapped and relaced with brandy occasionally, fruitcakes can keep for years.

dark FruitCake

3 lbs.	raisins
1 lb.	currants
1 lb.	dates, chopped
2 lbs.	mixed peel
2 cups	red and green candied cherries
1½ cups	blanched slivered almonds
12 oz.	brandy
2 cups	butter, softened
2 cups	sugar
9	eggs
4 cups	all-purpose flour
1 tsp.	EACH ground cloves, nutmeg, and ginger
2 tsp.	EACH cinnamon and salt
1 cup	molasses
1 tsp.	baking soda dissolved in 2 tsp. water
1 cup	grape juice
1 cup	grape jelly
	cheesecloth for wrapping cake
	extra brandy for sprinkling on cheesecloth

Place all the fruit and the almonds in a large bowl. Pour brandy over the fruit. Cover bowl and allow fruit to sit for several hours or overnight.

Preheat oven to 275°F. Grease and line with greased parchment paper several 3-4" deep pans. This recipe will make 2, 4½ x 8" loaves and 2, 9" tube pans.

Cream butter and sugar until light. Add eggs 1 at a time, beating well after each addition. In a separate bowl, combine flour and spices. Add molasses and baking soda to egg mixture. Add flour to egg mixture alternately with grape juice and jelly. Beat until smooth. Pour batter on top of brandy-soaked fruit and mix until all the fruit is incorporated. Pour batter into prepared pans. Bake for 2-4 hours. Baking time will vary with cake size. Remove cakes from the oven when a toothpick inserted in the center comes out clean. Cool in pans for 15-20 minutes then remove to cool completely on wire racks. Wrap cakes in brandy-soaked cloth then in aluminum foil. Be sure to wrap well; the flavor of these cakes improves with age. Store in a cool dry place.

Makes approximately 9-10 pounds of fruitcake. Fruitcakes may also be frozen.

P IES & T ARTS

Fresh Blueberry Pie, page 59
Strawberry Tarts, page 61

 54

Carrot Pudding

For many people Carrot Pudding has become their favorite Christmas Pudding tradition. My mother's favorite Christmas story was "A Christmas Carol". Every Christmas, Mom would pour brandy over the top of the pudding; do her Mrs. Crattchit impersonation, and carry the flaming pudding to the dinner table.

1 cup	grated raw carrot
1 cup	grated raw potato
½ cup	butter, softened
1 cup	white sugar
¾ cup	dark raisins
½ cup	currants
1-2 cups	deluxe candied cake fruit
1 cup	slivered almonds
1 cup	all-purpose flour, divided
½ tsp.	cloves
½ tsp.	nutmeg
½ tsp.	cinnamon
1 tsp.	baking soda

Grate carrots and potato. Measure and set aside.

Cream butter; add sugar and blend well. Add carrots and half the grated potato; mix well. Sprinkle fruit and almonds with ¼ cup of flour and add to the first mixture. Sift together the remaining flour and the spices. Stir into the carrot mixture. Dissolve baking soda in remaining ½ cup of potato and add last. Mix lightly. Pour into buttered bowls or molds. Cover well with foil and wrap with string to hold. Steam for 3 hours. If pudding is not going to be used immediately, wrap in plastic wrap and foil and refrigerate for 1 week or freeze up to 2 months. Defrost completely before the final steaming process.

Approximately 1 hour before serving, reheat pudding by steaming, once again, for approximately 1 hour.

Serve with rum sauce, page 56, or ice cream.

Serves 6-8. This recipe freezes well.

Rum Sauce

A buttery, rum-flavored sauce. It is wonderful served over ice cream, apple pie, or Christmas pudding.

1 cup	**water**
2 tbsp.	**light corn syrup**
¾ cup	**brown sugar**
¼ cup	**butter**
1½ tbsp.	**cornstarch**
⅓ cup	**rum**

Combine water, syrup, and brown sugar. Cook over low heat, stirring constantly, until sugar dissolves. Remove from heat and add butter and cornstarch. Return to heat and cook over moderate heat until sauce thickens. Stir frequently. When sauce has thickened, add the rum. Keep warm over low heat. Serve over ice cream or with carrot pudding.

Makes 2 cups of sauce.

Lemon Sauce

Serve this tangy sauce with angel food cake, bread puddings, or fresh fruit.

½ cup	**sugar**
1½ tbsp.	**cornstarch**
1 cup	**hot water**
¼ tsp.	**salt**
3 tbsp.	**fresh lemon juice**
2 tbsp.	**butter, softened**

Mix sugar and cornstarch together. Add hot water and whisk until smooth. Cook in microwave on high for about 5 minutes, or until thickened, stirring several times while cooking OR cook over boiling water or low heat, stirring constantly until thickened. Add salt and lemon juice. Cook 1 minute longer. Add butter, stir until melted. Cover and cool in refrigerator.

Makes 1½-2 cups of sauce.

Pies & Tarts

Single Pie Crust

1⅓ cups	all-purpose flour
½ tsp.	sugar
½ tsp.	salt
½ cup	all-vegetable shortening
3 tbsp.	cold water

To prepare pastry, combine flour, sugar, and salt in a medium bowl. Cut in shortening, using 2 knives scissor style, or a pastry blender, to form chunks the size of a pea. Sprinkle with water 1 tbsp. at a time. Toss lightly until pastry can be formed into a ball. Do not overmix. Wrap the ball well in waxed paper and place in refrigerator for a minimum of 6 hours. Remove pastry from refrigerator 1 hour before rolling.

To roll pastry, lightly flour working surface and rolling pin. Flatten dough between hands, place on floured work surface and roll from center outwards in all directions until of desired size. Trim pastry so it is 1½" larger all around than the upside-down pie plate. Roll pastry onto rolling pin and place in lightly greased 9 or 10" pie plate. Prick bottom and sides with fork to prevent shrinkage. Fill with the filling of your choice and bake according to filling directions.

To bake an unfilled pie crust, or bake it "blind", do not prick the crust; line it with waxed or parchment paper. Trim the edges so they don't stick up over the rim of the crust. Fill the crust with raw rice, uncooked beans, lentils, or pie weights. The weight of these "fillings" keeps the pastry from bubbling and shrinking away from the edge of the pie plate as it bakes. Bake at 425°F for 15 minutes. Remove the weights and paper. Bake empty pie crust at 375°F for 15-20 minutes, or until lightly browned.

Double Pie Crust

2 ⅓ cups	flour
1 tsp.	salt
1 tsp.	sugar
1 cup	all-vegetable shortening
7-8 tbsp.	water

Follow the preparation instructions above. Use the baking instructions appropriate to your filling.

Recipe makes 1, 9-10" double pie crust.

Fresh blueberry pie

Fresh firm blueberries and low-fat filling combine to make this a light summertime treat.

9"	baked pie crust, see page 58

Blueberry Filling:

4 cups	fresh blueberries
²⁄₃ cup	sugar
2 tbsp.	cornstarch
¼ cup	water
2 tbsp.	lemon juice

Creamy Low-Fat Cheese Filling:

½ cup	low-fat cottage cheese
1 tsp.	milk
1 tsp.	vanilla
1½ tbsp.	sugar
½ tsp.	lemon juice

Prepare the baked pie crust. To add visual interest, you may want to try a rough-textured-looking or free-form pie crust, as shown on page 53.

To prepare the blueberry filling, purée 2 cups of the blueberries in a blender or food processor. In a saucepan or microwave-proof bowl, combine sugar and cornstarch, stir in water, lemon juice, and puréed blueberries. Cook over medium heat on the stove or in the microwave until thick and clear. Remember to stir frequently. Remove from heat and cool.

To prepare the cheese filling, combine cottage cheese, milk, vanilla, sugar, and lemon juice and blend until smooth. Pour filling into prepared pie crust. Place remaining raw berries on top of filling.

Spoon glazed blueberry mixture over raw blueberries, making sure blueberries are totally covered. Refrigerate until serving. This pie is best when eaten the same day it is prepared.

Serves 6-8.

PICTURED ON PAGE 53.

fresh peach pie

A family summer favorite made with firm juicy peaches.

9-10" baked pie crust, see page 58

Peach Filling:

5	**fresh peaches, peeled, sliced**
⅔ cup	**sugar**
2 tbsp.	**cornstarch**
¼ cup	**water**
2 tbsp.	**lemon juice**

Prepare the baked pie crust.

To prepare the filling, purée 1 cup of the peach slices in a blender. In a saucepan or a microwave-proof bowl, combine sugar and cornstarch; stir in water, lemon juice, and puréed peaches. Cook peach mixture on medium until thick and clear. Remember to stir frequently. Place remaining peach slices in crust. Spoon glazed peach mixture over peach slices, making sure slices are totally covered. Refrigerate until serving. This pie is best when eaten the same day it is prepared. Serve plain or with ice cream.

Serves 6-8.

Mixed berry pie

pastry for 9" double, deep-dish pie, see page 58

Berry Filling:

1	**egg white**
2 tbsp.	**granulated sugar**
20 oz.	**bag of frozen mixed berries (600 g)***
¾ cup	**sugar**
1 tbsp.	**lemon juice**
2 tbsp.	**berry-flavored liqueur**
3 tbsp.	**cornstarch**
1½ tbsp.	**butter**

Mixed Berry Pie
(Continued)

Prepare pie pastry. Preheat oven to 425°F. Lightly grease pie plate. Place bottom crust in plate. Brush pastry with egg white and sprinkle with 1 tbsp. of the granulated sugar.

In a large bowl, combine the frozen berries, sugar, lemon juice, liqueur, and cornstarch. Toss well. Place berry mixture in prepared pie shell. Dot with butter. Cover with top pastry and pierce the top crust several times. Brush with remaining egg white and sprinkle with second tbsp. of granulated sugar. Place pie on foil-lined cookie sheet (berries tend to be quite juicy). Bake at 425°F for 10 minutes; reduce heat to 350°F and bake for 50-60 minutes, or until pastry is golden brown and filling appears to have thickened. Remove pie from oven and place on wire rack to cool.

Serves 6-8.

* Use fresh berries in season, but reduce cornstarch to 2 tbsp.

Strawberry Tarts

These tarts are easy to make and taste as good as they look.

12	**prebaked tart shells, see pastry page 58**
1-2 cups	**custard sauce, see page 69**
2	**baskets fresh strawberries**
½-¾ cup	**red currant jelly**
1 cup	**whipping cream**
¼ cup	**powdered (icing) sugar**

Prepare tarts shells or use commercial baked shells.

Prepare custard sauce.

Wash and hull strawberries and set aside to dry. Place jelly in a small saucepan and melt until liquid. In a medium bowl, whip cream and powdered sugar together and set aside. Spoon custard into baked shells, being careful not to overfill. Place strawberries, either whole or sliced, on top of custard. Brush or spoon melted jelly over strawberries so surface is covered. Garnish with whipped cream when ready to serve.

Serves 12.

PICTURED ON PAGE 53.

Almond Crunch Apple Pie

Almonds and brown sugar give a sweet crunchy taste to this traditional family favorite.

9"	single pie crust, unbaked, see page 58
5 cups	peeled sliced apples (preferably tart apples such as Spy, Granny Smith, OR MacIntosh)
⅔ cup	brown sugar
2 tbsp.	flour
1½ tbsp.	lemon juice
1 tsp.	cinnamon
1½ tbsp.	butter

Almond Brown Sugar Topping:

¼ cup	brown sugar
¼ cup	butter
½ cup	flour
½ tsp.	cinnamon
½ cup	sliced blanched almonds

Prepare pie crust. Preheat oven to 400°F.

In a large bowl, combine peeled apples, brown sugar, flour, lemon juice, and cinnamon. Toss until apples are well covered. Place in the pastry shell. Dot apples with butter.

To prepare the topping, combine all ingredients, except almonds, until they crumble. Sprinkle topping over apple mixture, followed by almonds. Bake at 400°F for 10 minutes then reduce heat to 350°F and bake for 35-45 minutes, or until apples are soft and pie is golden brown.

Serves 6-8.

 ## Apples

There are thousands of varieties of apples, they have been cultivated for over 3,000 years. For baking and cooking, use firm, flavorful apples such as Northern Spy, Granny Smith, Golden Delicious, MacIntosh, Baldwin, Cortland, Rome Beauty, or Winesap.

lemon Tarts

Lemon Curd is an excellent filling for tart shells. It can also be used as a filling for birthday cakes.

12	prebaked tart shells, see page 58

Lemon Curd:

¾ cup	sugar
2	whole eggs, beaten
2	egg yolks, beaten
½ cup	lemon juice
1½ tsp.	finely grated lemon rind
½ cup	butter, softened
1 cup	whipping cream
¼ cup	powdered sugar

Prepare tart shells. Make lemon curd ahead of time

To prepare lemon curd:

For microwave method, in a medium microwave-proof bowl, combine sugar, whole eggs, egg yolks, lemon juice, and lemon rind. Beat well. Microwave on medium for 5-7 minutes, beating after each minute. Do not microwave on high as eggs will cook too fast and mixture will be lumpy. Once mixture has thickened, stir in butter. Cover and cool in refrigerator.

For stovetop method, in the top of a double boiler, combine eggs, egg yolks, lemon juice, sugar, and lemon rind. Beat thoroughly. Cook over medium heat, stirring frequently. When mixture has thickened, remove from heat and stir in the butter. Cover and cool in the refrigerator.

Whip cream and powdered sugar together until soft peaks form. Fill tart shells with lemon curd. Garnish with whipped cream and serve.

Makes 12 tarts.

lemon Meringue pie

My mother loved lemons and always believed in using freshly squeezed lemon juice. This recipe was one of her favorites.

9"	**baked pie crust, see page 58**

Lemon Filling:

¼ cup	cornstarch
⅛ tsp.	salt
1 cup	sugar
1½ cups	boiling water
⅓ cup	lemon juice
1 tbsp.	finely grated lemon rind
2	egg yolks, beaten
2 tbsp.	butter

Meringue:

2	egg whites at room temperature
4 tbsp.	sugar
pinch	salt
½ tsp.	vanilla extract

Prepare pie crust.

To prepare the filling, mix cornstarch, salt, and sugar thoroughly in the top of a double boiler or in microwave-proof bowl. Add water, lemon juice, and rind and cook over simmering water, stirring constantly, or on medium in the microwave, stirring frequently, until thickened. Stir lemon mixture into beaten egg yolks and cook 1 minute longer. Stir in butter. Cool. Pour into baked pastry shell.

To prepare the meringue, beat egg whites until stiff. Add sugar gradually until mixture holds its shape. Add salt and vanilla. Spread the meringue evenly over the surface of the filling, being sure it touches the pastry rim all around. Bake at 325°F for 12-18 minutes, or until golden brown.

Serves 6-8.

CheeseCakes, puddings & pastries

raspberry Cheesecake

This recipe is best made a day ahead and garnished with the fresh raspberries and sauce the day it is to be served.

Raspberry Sauce or Coulis:

2 x 10 oz.	pkgs. (300 g) frozen unsweetened raspberries, thawed
1 cup	raspberry jelly
2 tbsp.	cornstarch
2 tbsp.	raspberry liqueur.

Chocolate Crust:

1 cup	chocolate cookie crumbs
3 tbsp.	melted butter

Raspberry Cheesecake:

3 x 8 oz.	pkgs. (250 g) cream cheese, softened
3	eggs
½ cup	sugar
¼ cup	raspberry sauce
2 cups	fresh raspberries for garnish

Prepare the sauce ahead of time. Combine thawed raspberries, jelly, cornstarch, and liqueur in a medium saucepan. Cook over medium heat until mixture thickens adequately to coat a metal spoon. Remove from heat and strain through a sieve. Allow to cool completely.

To prepare the crust, combine cookie crumbs and melted butter and press into the bottom of a 9" springform pan. Bake for 10 minutes at 350°F. Remove from oven.

To make the filling, beat the cream cheese until soft; add eggs 1 at a time and beat until smooth. Add sugar and ¼ cup of raspberry sauce. Mix until well blended. Pour mixture into prepared cheesecake pan. Bake at 350°F for approximately 35-40 minutes, or until set. Turn off oven and open oven door. Allow cheesecake to cool in oven until it can be handled without oven mitts. Remove from oven and run a knife around the edge of the pan. Chill cheesecake in refrigerator before removing from pan. Garnish with fresh raspberries. Spoon remaining raspberry sauce over raspberries. Chill until ready to serve.

Serves 8-10.

Amaretto Cheesecake

The rich subtle flavor of amaretto in a creamy cheesecake is a lovely contrast to the crunch of the toasted almonds.

Crust:

3 tbsp.	butter
⅓ cup	sugar
1	egg
¾ cup	flour

Amaretto Cheesecake Filling:

3 x 8 oz.	pkgs. (250 g) of cream cheese, softened
3	eggs
½ cup	sugar
⅓ cup	amaretto
	whipping cream for garnish
⅓ cup	toasted sliced almonds

To prepare the crust, lightly grease a 9" springform pan and line with a parchment circle. Cream butter and sugar together. Add the egg, then the flour. Blend well. Press mixture into prepared cake pan. Bake at 350°F for 10 minutes. Remove from oven and set aside.

To prepare the cheesecake filling, cream softened cheese until light. Add eggs, blending well, then add the sugar, followed by the amaretto. Mix until smooth. Pour over base and bake at 350°F for 30-40 minutes, or until set. Turn off oven, open oven door slightly and allow cheesecake to cool in oven. Remove cake from oven and run a knife around the inside of the pan. Chill in the refrigerator. Before serving remove from pan and garnish with whipped cream. Sprinkle with toasted almonds.

Serves 8-10.

VARIATION: Drizzle melted chocolate over the almonds.

Turtle Cheesecake

Use the Caramel Sauce to fill cakes, bars, or cheesecakes.

Chocolate Crust:

1 cup	crushed chocolate cookie crumbs
3 tbsp.	melted butter

Caramel Sauce:

½ x 10 oz.	can (300 mL) sweetened condensed milk
½ cup	butter
2 tbsp.	corn syrup
½ cup	packed brown sugar
½ cup	chopped pecans

Chocolate Cheesecake Filling:

3 x 8 oz.	pkgs. (250 g) cream cheese, softened
½ cup	sugar
3	eggs
4 oz.	semisweet chocolate
	pecans, chocolate, and whipped cream for garnish

Preheat oven to 350°F. Lightly grease a 9" cheesecake pan. Line the bottom with a circle of parchment paper.

To prepare the crust, combine cookie crumbs and melted butter; press into prepared pan. Bake for 10 minutes. Remove from oven; set aside.

To make the caramel sauce, combine all ingredients in a medium saucepan. Cook over medium heat. When mixture begins to boil continue cooking for a full 5 minutes, stirring constantly. Remove pan from heat and pour caramel mixture over cooled base. Sprinkle with pecans.

To prepare the cheesecake filling, beat softened cream cheese until light. Add eggs and beat until smooth. Add sugar and melted chocolate. Blend well. Pour mixture over caramel. Bake at 350°F for 35-40 minutes, or until cake is set. Turn off oven, open oven door slightly and allow cheesecake to cool in oven. Remove from oven and run a knife around the sides of the pan. Chill in refrigerator. Before serving remove from pan and garnish with pecans, drizzled chocolate, and whipped cream.

Serves 8-10.

PICTURED ON PAGE 71.

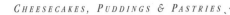

fresh berry Trifle

Mixed fresh berries add lovely color and flavor to this traditional, creamy English classic. It's a beautiful and luscious dessert year round.

9"	round sponge OR other white cake
¼ cup	sherry

Custard Sauce:

¼ cup	butter
½ cup	sugar
3	egg yolks
1 cup	cereal cream (half and half)
½ cup	milk
1½ tbsp.	cornstarch
1 tsp.	vanilla

1 cup	whipping cream
¼ cup	powdered sugar
3 cups	mixed fresh berries
	toasted almonds

To prepare custard:

For microwave method, in a medium microwave-proof bowl, melt butter. Cool. Add sugar and egg yolks; beat well. Next add the cream, milk, and cornstarch. Beat until well combined. Microwave on medium for 7-10 minutes, beating after 1½ minutes. When custard has thickened add vanilla. Cool completely and chill in the refrigerator.

For stove top method, in the top of a double boiler, over simmering water, combine butter, sugar, and egg yolks; beat well. Add the cream, milk, and cornstarch. Beat until well blended. Cook over medium heat until thickened. Stir frequently. When custard has thickened add vanilla. Cool in the refrigerator.

Beat whipping cream and powdered sugar together until stiff peaks form.

To assemble, place sponge cake in a trifle dish or a clear glass bowl. Sprinkle the sherry over the sponge cake. Spread custard over the sponge cake. Spoon fresh berries over the custard, saving a few berries for garnish. Spoon or pipe the whipping cream on top of the berries and garnish with toasted almonds and fresh berries. Chill until serving.

Serves 6-8.

Swan Cream Puffs

Don't be intimidated. These are easy to make and they look beautiful - your family and friends will love them.

Choux Paste:

1 cup	boiling water
½ cup	butter, softened
1 cup	flour
4	eggs
2 cups	whipping cream
⅓ cup	powdered sugar

Have water boiling. Add butter to water in a small smooth saucepan and place over heat. When butter is melted and mixture is boiling vigorously, dump in flour all at once. Stir rapidly until mixture makes a ball and comes away from the sides of the pan. Do not overcook. Remove from heat and add eggs 1 at a time, beating thoroughly after each addition. Beat until batter does not stick to blade when cut through with a knife.

Lightly grease 2 cookie sheets.

Using a pastry bag with a plain tip and approximately ⅓ of the dough, pipe question marks on an ungreased cookie sheet to form the heads and necks of the swans. Bake the necks in a 400°F oven for 10 minutes, or until golden brown. Remove from oven and cool. Next, using a pastry bag with a serrated or star tip, pipe 3" puffs on an ungreased cookie sheet. Bake at 400°F for 10 minutes. Reduce heat to 350°F and continue to bake for approximately 25 minutes. Allow puffs to cool in oven until they are firm to the touch. Remove puffs from oven and cool completely, away from drafts.

To fill, slice the tops off the puffs and slice the tops lengthwise; these 2 pieces will form the wings of the swan. Next, remove any damp dough pieces left inside the bottom of the puff.

Beat whipping cream and powdered sugar together until stiff peaks form. Fill the puff bottoms with whipped cream and position neck and wing pieces to create the desired effect. Serve the same day.

Serves 8-12.

72

dessert rosettes or Timbales

Rosettes are a light and crunchy dessert pastry. They may be served on their own or as an accompaniment for fruit salad. My grandmother Moore, my father's mother, made these when I was a child, as did my mother. The rosettes are light but sweet and were a particular favorite of mine when I was growing up.

2	eggs
2 tsp.	white sugar
¼ tsp.	salt
1 tbsp.	lemon extract
1 cup	milk
1 cup	all-purpose flour
	rosette iron*
	oil for deep frying
½-1 cup	powdered (icing) sugar

Beat eggs, sugar, salt, and lemon extract together until smooth. Stir milk and flour alternately into egg mixture. Beat until smooth.

Pour vegetable oil into a deep-fryer to a depth of 3". Heat oil to 325-350°F. Prepare rosette iron by dipping it into the hot oil. Next dip the iron into the batter, being careful not to allow the batter to run over the top of the iron. Immerse batter-covered iron in hot oil for 25-35 seconds. Remove rosette from iron using a fork. Allow rosettes to drain on paper towels and repeat process using the rest of the batter. Dust finished rosettes with icing sugar.

VARIATION: Add cinnamon to the icing sugar for added flavor.

* Rosette irons can be found in specialty kitchen shops. They may be shaped like flowers, stars, hearts, or butterflies, etc. Timbale irons come in shapes like the rosette irons, but they are usually used to create pastry shells that are filled with a sweet or savory filling.

brandied almond & pecan baklava

My sister-in-law, Maria, gave me this recipe. She moved to Canada from Greece at the age of 13 and has many wonderful recipes for Greek dishes which our whole family loves. Maria is a favorite of our youngest son, Scott. He calls her Auntie Miya.

Honey Syrup:

1½ cups	sugar
1 cup	honey
3 cups	water
10-12	whole cloves

Brandied Almond Pecan Filling:

3 cups	coarsely chopped almonds
2 cups	coarsely chopped pecans
⅔ cup	crushed Holland rusks
2 tbsp.	sugar
1 tsp.	cinnamon
1 tsp.	cloves
2 tsp.	allspice
2 tbsp.	brandy
1 lb.	butter
½ cup	oil
2 x 1 lb.	pkgs. (2 x 454 g) of phyllo pastry, thawed

To prepare the syrup, combine sugar, honey, water, and cloves in a saucepan. Stir until sugar and honey dissolve. Bring to a gentle boil and cook for ½ hour. Remove from heat and allow syrup to cool completely. Remove cloves and refrigerate syrup.

For the filling, combine all filling ingredients in a large bowl.

To assemble, melt the butter and oil together in a medium saucepan. Using a pastry brush, brush a small amount of butter mixture in the bottom of a 14" square pan or an 11 x 15" cake pan. Place 1 sheet of phyllo pastry in the bottom of the pan. It may have to be trimmed depending on the size of the pan used. Brush butter on phyllo and repeat with next piece of pastry. Follow procedure until 10 pieces have been layered with butter.

brandied almond & pecan baklava

(Continued)

Sprinkle a layer of the nut filling on the top sheet, followed by a sheet of phyllo. Brush phyllo with butter. Add another sheet of pastry and brush with butter. Add a third sheet of pastry and brush with butter. Sprinkle with another layer of the nut mixture and repeat the procedure until all the nut mixture has been used. Layer the rest of the phyllo, each sheet brushed with butter, on top of the final layer of nut mixture.

Score the pastry ¾ of the way through, cutting diagonally in the shape of diamonds. Bake at 350°F for approximately 45 minutes, or until golden brown. Remove from oven; while hot, pour cooled syrup over the pastry. Allow to cool completely. Cut bars the rest of way through and store.

Makes 24-30 pieces.

PICTURED ON PAGE 71.

baked apple crisp

Very easy, very good, and very versatile!

3 cups	thinly sliced apples
¼ cup	flour
¼ cup	quick rolled oats
¾ cup	brown sugar
¼ cup	butter
½ cup	slivered almonds

Arrange apples in a buttered 9 or 10" round casserole. Combine flour, oats, and brown sugar. Cut in butter until size of small peas; add nuts and sprinkle evenly over the apples. Bake at 350°F for 40-50 minutes, until apples are tender. Serve warm or cold with cream or ice cream.

Serves 4-6.

VARIATIONS: Most fresh fruits, alone or in combination, are superb in this recipe. Try rhubarb or rhubarb and strawberries, peaches or peaches and blueberries, pears, apricots, nectarines, etc. A tbsp. of lemon juice brings out the fruit flavors. Tart fruit, such as rhubarb, should be combined with about ½ cup of sugar. If you love cinnamon, add 1-2 tsp. of cinnamon to the topping.

Sugar—Glazed Spudnuts

Spudnuts are potato-based yeast doughnuts. Mom Weatherby's are the best. She made these when my husband, Glenn, and his brothers were growing up. After I was married she passed the recipe on to me and our eldest son, Blaine, loves them as much as his father does.

1½ tbsp.	dry yeast (2 envelopes)
½ cup	water
½ tsp.	sugar
4 cups	scalded milk, cooled
1 cup	butter
1 cup	sugar
5	eggs, beaten
2 cups	mashed potatoes
1½ tsp.	salt
2 tsp.	nutmeg
3-4 cups	flour

Glaze:

2 cups	icing sugar
2 tbsp.	butter, softened
¼ cup	hot water, approximately

Dissolve yeast in water and ½ tsp. sugar. Add yeast to cooled scalded milk. Cream butter, sugar, eggs, potatoes, salt, and nutmeg. Add yeast and milk to creamed mixture. Add enough flour to make a soft dough. Cover and let rise in a warm place, until double in size. On a floured surface, knead dough and roll about ½" thick. Cut with a doughnut cutter and let rise again. Cook doughnuts in deep hot oil, about 365°F, until golden brown.

Make glaze, by combining icing sugar and butter, and stirring in enough water to make it fairly thin. Dip spudnuts in glaze while they are still warm.

Makes 3-4 dozen spudnuts.

Mom's Sticky Buns

As children, my brother and I loved it when our mom made buns.
She always used a sweet bun base, doubled or tripled the recipe, and
made delicious "sticky" buns with part of the recipe. These are best
eaten the day they are made.

2 tbsp.	dry yeast
1 cup	lukewarm water
2 tsp.	sugar
1 cup	milk
¼ cup	butter, softened
½ cup	sugar
1 tsp.	salt
6 cups	all-purpose flour
2	eggs, beaten
½ cup	melted butter
1 cup	brown sugar
3 tbsp.	cinnamon

Sticky Topping:

½ cup	melted butter
1 cup	brown sugar
3 tbsp.	light corn syrup
1 cup	chopped pecans (optional)

Soften yeast in lukewarm water and 2 tsp. sugar. Scald milk; add butter, ½ cup sugar, and salt. Cool until lukewarm. Add half of the flour to make a thick batter. Add eggs. Add enough flour to make a soft dough. Knead until satiny, about 10-15 minutes. Place dough in a greased bowl and turn to coat all over. Cover with a damp tea towel. Let rise until double in bulk, about 30 minutes. Punch down dough. Roll into a large rectangle. Pour melted butter on the dough and sprinkle with brown sugar and cinnamon. Roll dough lengthwise, jelly-roll style. Preheat oven to 375°F. Lightly grease an 11 x 15" cake pan or 2, 9" cake pans. Combine ingredients for topping and sprinkle in prepared pan. Slice roll into 2" rounds. Cover with a damp tea towel and let rise until almost double in bulk, about 30 minutes. Bake for 25-30 minutes. Remove from oven and let cool for 10 minutes before inverting onto waxed paper or cooling rack.

Makes 12-18 large buns.

banana bread

A childhood favorite, this moist banana loaf has a slightly nutty flavor.

1 cup	sugar
½ cup	butter, softened
2	eggs
3	bananas, mashed
1 cup	flour
⅓ cup	hazelnut flour (available at specialty health food stores)
½ tsp.	baking powder
1 tsp.	baking soda
	pinch of salt

Combine all ingredients in the order given. Spoon the batter into a lightly greased 3 x 5 x 9" loaf pan. Bake at 325°F for approximately 1 hour and 15 minutes.

Makes 1 loaf. This bread freezes well.

porcupines

This is another childhood favorite of my husband's, passed onto me by his mother.

2 cups	white sugar
½ cup	milk
½ cup	butter (slightly less)
1 tsp.	vanilla
pinch	salt
¼ cup	cocoa
1 cup	coconut
3 cups	oatmeal

Combine the first 6 ingredients in a large saucepan. Bring to a boil over medium heat. Boil for 3 minutes. Remove from heat and add coconut and oatmeal. Drop by spoonfuls onto waxed paper and cool.

Makes 3-4 dozen.

Confections

White Chocolate Truffles

The truffles we made in our shop were a small side item we added to our menu but they became one of the biggest selling items we had.

1¼ lbs.	white chocolate (couverture)*
⅞ cup	whipping cream
1⅓ cup	butter, softened
	flavorings: e.g., peppermint extract, amaretto, Grand Marnier, undiluted concentrated orange juice, coconut extract, sour cherries, Kahlúa, etc.
1 lb.	high-grade milk chocolate (couverture)*

Melt the white chocolate in the top of a double boiler. Melt slowly on low to medium heat or chocolate will burn or become lumpy. Scald cream and set aside. When chocolate is completely melted, remove from heat and beat in cooled cream and softened butter. Beat until mixture is smooth and all ingredients are incorporated. Place the bowl of truffle mixture in the refrigerator until cool but not cold to the touch. Beat once again. The cream is ready for flavorings once it changes from a yellowish appearance to a creamy white and soft peaks can be formed. Do not over-beat. Transfer the cream into 3 separate bowls and add your favorite flavorings. Be careful not to add anything with too much water content (e.g. frozen strawberries, etc). Oil flavorings work well as not much is needed. A tbsp. of liqueur such as Kahlúa or amaretto work well. Cover and place bowls of creams in refrigerator. Allow to chill until firm enough for balls to be formed. To make balls use a melon baller (preferably with a release mechanism). Place balls in a waxed paper-lined container. Cover balls and freeze until ready to dip. If you are using good-quality pure couverture for dipping it will be necessary for you to temper the milk chocolate before dipping the truffles. Pure couverture contains no wax, unlike much of the North American chocolate. See page 81.

Dip truffles, using a dipping spoon or a pickle or carving fork (two-tined),and garnish as desired. Store in a moisture-free refrigerator in covered containers. ***Makes 50-60 truffles.***

PICTURED ON PAGE 35.

* Couverture is a professional-quality high cocoa-butter chocolate used for coatings. Found in specialty candy-making shops and some bulk food stores, it forms a very thin smooth shell or coating.

Tempering Couverture

*Pure chocolate or couverture does not contain waxes or palm oils.
Cocoa butter should be one of the first ingredients listed.*

Tempering is the process of heating chocolate and cooling it to precise temperatures so that the fat in the cocoa butter crystallizes. If the chocolate has been well tempered it will be shiny in appearance and snap once set. One method of tempering is to break the chocolate into small pieces and melt it in the top of a double boiler over simmering, not boiling, water. You will need a chocolate thermometer for accurate testing of the temperature. In the first stage the pure chocolate is heated to 115°F. Next, remove the pot from the hot water and place the pot in a bowl of cold water, being careful not to get any water into the chocolate. Stir the couverture until it reaches 80-82°F. Return the pan to the hot water and heat to 88°F. Milk chocolate should be heated 2°F lower in all 3 stages. Now you are ready to dip. To test whether the tempering was successful, place a small drop on a piece of waxed paper; if it sets up within 3 minutes and remains shiny, the tempering is a success. Keep the temperature in the room where you are dipping below 70°F to allow the chocolate to set properly.

Another method of tempering is to heat the chocolate to 115°F, remove from heat and pour ⅔ of the chocolate onto a marble slab. Work the chocolate using a plastic scraper and a "S" motion to bring down the temperature. Once the chocolate begins to set up, return it to the pot, mixing it with the other chocolate. Reheat the chocolate to 88°F and dip the truffles or chocolates.

NOTES: It is best to find European chocolate, if possible, as most of the North American chocolate contains additives such as oils.

Tempering should be done on all pure couverture, whether it is dark, milk, or white chocolate, if it is to be used for dipping.

brandy, amaretto, and rum Truffles

These are superb, rich and creamy, they literally melt in your mouth.

Truffle Cream:

1¼ lbs.	semisweet couverture (chocolate)
⅞ cup	whipping cream
1⅓ cups	butter, softened
1½ tbsp.	EACH of brandy, rum, and amaretto
	OR flavor according to your taste

1 lb.	milk chocolate (couverture) for dipping
	chopped pecans
	chopped toasted almonds
½ cup	sifted unsweetened cocoa
½ cup	powdered sugar

For truffle cream, break semisweet chocolate and melt in a double boiler or a bowl over simmering water. Scald whipping cream and set aside to cool. When chocolate is melted, remove from heat and beat in cream followed by softened butter. Blend well. Divide truffle cream into 3 bowls and add flavorings. Cover bowls and chill in refrigerator for several hours, or until quite firm to the touch. Using a melon baller, form the truffle cream into balls. Place balls in a waxed paper-lined container; cover and freeze until ready to dip.

For dipping, melt and temper milk chocolate, see page 81 if using pure couverture. Combine powdered sugar and unsweetened cocoa in a small bowl. Place chopped pecans and almonds in 2 separate bowls.

Dip **Rum Truffles** in milk chocolate; roll while wet in powdered sugar mixture and set aside on wax paper to dry.

Dip **Brandy Truffles** in milk chocolate; roll while wet in pecans.

Dip **Amaretto Truffles** and roll in toasted almonds.

Store truffles in covered containers in the refrigerator.

Makes 50-60 truffles.

PICTURED ON PAGE 35.

milk Chocolate Truffles

⅞ cup	**whipping cream**
1¼ lbs.	**milk chocolate (couverture)**
1¼ cups	**butter, softened**
1 lb.	**milk chocolate (couverture) for dipping**

Scald cream and set aside to cool. Break 1¼ lbs. of milk chocolate into small pieces and melt in a bowl or double boiler over simmering water. Remove chocolate from heat and mix in cooled cream followed by softened butter. Beat until well blended. Pour into a bowl and cover. Chill in refrigerator several hours, or until the cream is stiff enough to be formed into balls. To make balls use a melon baller with a release mechanism. Place balls in a waxed paper-lined container. Cover and put in freezer until time to dip. To dip truffles either a dipping spoon (available at craft or some specialty food stores) or a carving fork can be used. Store truffles in a covered container in refrigerator. Do not store close to foods such as onions as smells can be transferred.

Makes 50-60 truffles.

PICTURED ON PAGE 35.

rich Toffee

This is a rich buttery toffee that is also excellent with a layer of melted chocolate on top.

3 cups	**packed brown sugar**
1 cup	**butter**
10 oz.	**can (300 mL) sweetened condensed milk**
1 cup	**light corn syrup**

Put all ingredients into a large heavy saucepan. Bring to a boil over medium heat and cook to 290°F, hard crack stage*, stirring constantly. This will take a long time, approximately 45 minutes. Candy will turn dark brown during cooking. It will burn easily so be sure to stir constantly.

Pour toffee onto a large lightly buttered cookie sheet. When cool break into pieces.

Makes approximately 1 pound of toffee.

* If you prefer chewy toffee rather than brittle, cook to 240°F.

homemade marshmallows

Your children will be VERY impressed that YOU can make marshmallows.

2 tbsp.	gelatin
1½ cups	water
2 cups	sugar
1 tsp.	vanilla
⅛ tsp.	salt
	powdered sugar, coconut OR crushed cornflakes for coating

Soak gelatin in ¾ cup of the water. With other ½ of the water make a syrup by adding sugar. Stir until dissolved; cook over medium heat to softball stage, 235°F. Add the soaked gelatin to the boiled mixture. Let stand until partly cooled; add vanilla and salt. With an electric mixer, beat gelatin mixture until it becomes white and fluffy or thick, about 15 minutes. Dust a shallow 8-9" square cake pan with powdered sugar and pour mixture into pan. Let candy set; loosen edges with a knife; turn out onto a cutting board. Cut into cubes, roll in powdered sugar, coconut, or crushed cornflakes.

Makes 36, 1½ x 1½" marshmallows.

NOTE: *This recipe requires a great amount of beating to make it fluffy.*

VARIATIONS: To make colored marshmallows, add a few drops of food color.

peanut brittle

2 cups	granulated sugar
1 cup	light corn syrup
½ cup	water
1 cup	butter
2 cups	salted peanuts
1 tsp.	baking soda

Over medium heat, stir sugar, syrup, and water in a large saucepan until sugar dissolves. When syrup begins to boil, blend in butter. Using a candy thermometer, cook mixture, stirring often after it reaches 230°F. Add nuts at 275°F and stir constantly to hard crack stage, 305°F. Remove from heat; quickly add baking soda, mixing well. Pour brittle mixture onto a large lightly buttered cookie sheet and stretch thin using 2 forks. Loosen from cookie sheet and break into pieces when cool.

 Makes about 1 pound of peanut brittle.

Index

ʃɦare rɪcɦ rewardʃ

*Order **Rich Rewards** at $9.95 per book plus $3.00 (total order) for postage and handling.*

Number of books _____ x $9.95 = $_____

Shipping and handling charge _____ = _$___3.00___

Subtotal _____ = _$_____

In Canada add 7% GST _____ (Subtotal x .07) = _$_____

Total enclosed _____ = _$_____

U.S. and international orders payable in U.S. funds/Price is subject to change.

NAME:_____

STREET: _____

CITY:_____ PROV./STATE _____

COUNTRY _____ POSTAL CODE/ZIP _____

Please make cheque or money order payable to: Rich Rewards Publishing
Heather Heather
323 – 9 Street S.E.
Medicine Hat, Alberta
Canada   T1A 1N4

For fund raising or volume purchase prices, contact
Rich Rewards Publishing. Please allow 3-4 weeks for delivery.

ʃɦare rɪcɦ rewardʃ

*Order **Rich Rewards** at $9.95 per book plus $3.00 (total order) for postage and handling.*

Number of books _____ x $9.95 = $_____

Shipping and handling charge _____ = _$___3.00___

Subtotal _____ = _$_____

In Canada add 7% GST _____ (Subtotal x .07) = _$_____

Total enclosed _____ = _$_____

U.S. and international orders payable in U.S. funds/Price is subject to change.

NAME:_____

STREET: _____

CITY:_____ PROV./STATE _____

COUNTRY _____ POSTAL CODE/ZIP _____

Please make cheque or money order payable to: Rich Rewards Publishing
Heather Heather
323 – 9 Street S.E.
Medicine Hat, Alberta
Canada   T1A 1N4

For fund raising or volume purchase prices, contact
Rich Rewards Publishing. Please allow 3-4 weeks for delivery.